# Wal-Mart Book of Ethics
# Abridged Edition

## R.A. Wilson

**Shouldn't You Be Reading?**

AlyMur Productions ™

**This is an excellent read. I laughed to tears... Highly recommend reading this...**
-a.seas | Amazon.com Customer Review

**This short Kindle offering turned out to be an often-witty surprise.**
-John Williamson | Goodreads.com Review

**Really enjoyed reading this. Would like to read more. Actually laughed out loud. Please write more.**
-Vicki Coble Tucker | Amazon.com Customer Review

**Everything I read is so true especially the part about customers just expect service with a smile.**
-Jennifer | Amazon.com Customer Review

**These short vignettes will have you shaking your head, rolling your eyes, and wondering how some people manage to survive their own stupidity. The stories are silly, shocking, funny, and sometimes just plain nuts and will have you wondering if WalMart is part of a bizarro universe rather than a place firmly rooted in our own world.**
-Nyssa | Amazon.com Customer Review

Published by AlyMur Productions™
AlyMur.com

Copyright 2012 by R.A. Wilson
Discover other titles by R.A. Wilson at RavinSaga.com

ISBN-10: 0615792251
ISBN-13: 978-0615792255
ASIN: B007TCQO66

# Books by R.A. Wilson

## Ravin Saga

<u>The World of Ildor</u>
*Endospore*

## Shakespeare Novelizations

*The Tragedy of Macbeth*

## Other

*Wal-Mart Book of Ethics Abridged Edition*

To Wal-Mart for not checking how long we were on break, allowing us the time to write this book.

And also for Scooter, who is no longer with us.
This book is for you.

# Table of Contents

# Note

All events contained herein are real, either personally experienced or taken from firsthand accounts, but they did not necessarily happen in the order portrayed here. Names are written within, and they have not been changed to protect the innocent, because these people are not innocent. They are adults and are responsible for their actions, as are we all.

# Forward

There are numerous reasons to write this book. For me, it comes down to how much I hate working retail but love writing. This was bound to happen.

Once I had the idea, it seemed a stroke of brilliance, but even then, it took James' excitement to prompt me to write as I mostly read and write epic fantasy. This book also would not make my reading list, because I would think it exploitive. But this book is not like that. It is not a sellout but a coming to terms with a part of my life.

Most depictions of Wal-Mart take an anti or pro stance. Neither is accurate. Pro Wal-Mart works proclaim the positive aspects of the company, but they fail to show the whole picture. Anti Wal-Mart works are mostly lies, crafted purely as money makers for the producers, writers, and directors. In fact, while working for the company, I have watched anti Wal-Mart movies just for a good laugh as they are so misleading.

Ultimately, the point of this book is to show an accurate depiction of working in the retail environment. As this book is based on personal observations, it cannot tell you about the company as a whole, but rather of the store in which submitters work or shop. This is a book of experiences, not unfounded opinions.

On top of this, my intent is making this book entertaining

while never forgetting to stay as accurate as possible. Unfortunately, the nature of this book does skew the true experience of working retail. A completely accurate depiction would be boring and redundant, and perhaps become the second leading cause of suicide, right after college football.

In the end, this book boils down to a testament of how abnormal any retail environment is, be it Wal-Mart, Kmart, Sears, Target, Mc Donald's, Best Buy, etc. This is a look at how the abnormal becomes normal in the daily setting of retail sales. People can be kind and courteous, but in a retail store as customers, workers, or managers, everything changes. All bets are off.

It's funny 'cause it's true.

# Wal-Mart is dead!
# Long live Wal-Mart!

**By R.A. Wilson**

It is March 13, 2005. My college graduation is in two months, the Sony PSP releases tomorrow, and today is the grand opening of the new Wal-Mart Supercenter. The old store was closed yesterday at 6 pm to allow last-minute work to be done for opening day. Wal-Mart is dead! Long live Wal-Mart!

Hired as a cashier for the opening supercenter, one would expect me to work as such on opening day, the busiest day the store is to see. But reaching the front of the store, I find every register in use. This does not bode well, and the warm fuzzy feelings begin to die, but I try to not let it show in my demeanor. CSM Elvira, a Customer Service Manager, looks over the cashier list and says, "None of the cashiers need a break now, so I don't have a register for you." She looks at me and smiles. "Would you push carts for a while? We're backed up outside as there is only one courtesy associate here. She can use some help."

Though there is an overabundance of cashiers today, elsewhere we are short, and cake taster is apparently not one of those areas. "I guess I can," I respond, realizing I am to become the sacrificial lamb. I like to think this is because I am trusted to work beyond my job code, or maybe I am neanderthalish and good for physical labor; either way, I drew the proverbial short straw. As I head outside, I notice there are almost no available shopping carts at the doors for customers to use. They cannot all be in the store, leaving little wonder where they would be otherwise.

In the chilly air outside, I quickly observe the parking lot. The lights are coming on as the sun sets, and almost every parking spot is claimed. Cars are driving about, some leaving, and others looking for an open place to park within walking distance of the doors. I then notice the shopping cart corrals. They are so overfilled that the two rows of carts in each corral protrude over halfway through the driving lanes. I no longer wonder where the carts have disappeared to.

The cars are still driving through the lanes blocked by carts; they just drive around them, making the parking lot an obstacle course or an easy maze. It is obvious an accident is not long off, either from someone hitting the shopping carts, two cars hitting head on, a pedestrian being run over, or somebody trying to cross a line to cheat the maze. I understand why Elvira asked me to push carts, but is it really expected of two people to clear up this pile? I head into the parking lot, knowing my contemplations are not moving a single cart.

Not trained on the use of electric cart pushers, I have to push the shopping carts by hand. I find ten carts are the most I can safely push at a time, allowing me to push them uphill while still handling their bulk. It takes me four trips just to get the carts from one corral out of the lane, and four more to empty the corral completely. Eight trips per corral at three minutes per trip on average, and there are about fifteen corrals. I start on the south side of the parking lot, while the courtesy associate is on the north. We do not meet until we reach the middle of the lot.

She waves hi, and I wave back, but not as energetically. I see she is using one of the electric cart pushers. I am surprised by this as we cleared carts at the same pace when she should have been much faster with the cart pusher, being able to take three times the number of carts I can each trip. Unwilling to start conversation, I turn and start heading back through the corrals I already cleared, and she does the same. They are already filling, and by the time I reach the far south again, it is almost as bad as before I started. I feel like a salmon trying to swim up Niagara Falls.

I spend my first four hours outside, finally heading to lunch when another courtesy associate comes to work. After lunch, I hope to be placed on a register to do my actual job.

Back at the store front, CSM Kelly tells me there is no one working maintenance tonight, and she needs a spill cleaned.

"How interesting," I respond. "So, what register is mine?" It comes as a big surprise when she said there was not any available. She wants me to clean the spill instead. A customer dropped a jug of cleaning detergent at one of the self-checkouts, and Kelly admits making the spill worse by spreading it farther in attempting to clean it. She thanks me for taking her burden and walks away, much like Atlas to Hercules. I stand there, stuttering my complaint, unable to articulate my despondence. Maybe I should tell her I need a pillow for my sore shoulders and run away.

I see Kelly already poured Allsorb on the spill, our kitty litter-like spill absorbing cleaner. I add more as it is still a sticky clump and scrub with a broom to mix it thoroughly. I try to sweep it up, finding the Allsorb clumps together and rolls from under the broom instead of being swept along. I have to sweep the five-foot diameter area numerous times, each pass leaving the floor looking almost as it did before. I get on my hands and knees with a hand broom and go over the whole area once more to get the rest. That almost works, though it spots my light tan pants on the knees. Using a dust pan, I

8

bag the clumpy Allsorb. I stand to walk away and slip on the floor, nearly tumbling to the ground. A greasy residue still remains, which I realize will need a mop and bucket to remove. I place a wet floor sign on the area.

Assistant Manager Russ walks by me now and says, "Hey, when you're done with that, could you clean the bathrooms?"

I laugh at first but then notice he is being serious. "I'm a cashier," I respond. "A CSM asked me to clean this mess. I'm going to need to get on a register after this."

"That doesn't matter. Just take care of the bathrooms for me." Russ walks away before I can mouth further argument. I do not understand why no one seems to hear what I say.

I retrieve the mop and bucket after searching for a good twenty minutes, as nobody seems to know where they are located. I mop the residue, making it even more slippery until it completely dries. I end up standing there for about five minutes before I can even move on. During this time, numerous customers walk by, glaring at me for not running a register for them. A few customers even voice their frustration when seeing my name badge marks me a cashier. They seem to think that I should not be cleaning up messes instead of cashiering, though they do not seem to care that I agree, making me still at fault.

I put the mop and bucket away and talk to CSM Anna. "Russ asked me to clean the bathrooms. I was wondering if you needed me on a register instead."

"We're fine." She smiles at me, though shooing me off would have felt nicer. She was smiling warmly, but her eyes felt mocking.

I trudge off to the back of the store to get the bathroom cleaning cart, and I start with the men's restroom by layaway. I am grateful to see nothing smeared on the walls, because I half expected that, though it would have remained there. I am not paid that much. There is paper litter on the floor instead, which I sweep up and bag with the garbage. I clean the mirror and mop the floor, though I leave the toilets and urinals. I do not want this job that badly.

At the woman's restroom, I end up standing at the door for fifteen minutes before entering, but that is because women constantly push aside my cart blocking the doorway to bar entrance. I am not allowed in there if any woman is inside, so I have to wait for these impatient people to finish. I try to imagine what it would be like if our roles were reversed, giving me a small chuckle. When I get inside the restroom, I am further surprised. If women are the fairer sex, why is their bathroom dirtier?

They too have paper littering the floor, but it is more than double the men's restroom. The garbage cans are overflowing, and paper towels are clogging two of the sinks. The mirror here is smeared with...actually, I do not know what it is. All I know is I do

10

not want to touch it. I put on gloves to clean the mirror, and whatever is on the mirror is like a thick gel that sticks to the glass. I end up using half the bottle of window cleaner before I give up, far from satisfied.

I grab the paper towels from the sinks and throw them in the garbage cans before starting to sweep the floor. Not only is there more paper litter in here, but the paper is ripped into tatters like confetti, as if they have been tread on repeatedly. I sweep the floor, empty the garbage cans, and begin mopping. I start at the farthest point from the door, in the last stall, and notice something I missed while sweeping. There are small garbage receptacles in each stall, hanging on the walls. I am confused at first, but that quickly passes.

I have extensively studied physiology and anatomy in college, so I know more about circadian rhythms than most women, and menstrual cycles fall into such a category. Though I understand much, I am nevertheless surprised to see these receptacles and feel foolish for this. I prop the mop against the wall and open the first one and take out the bag inside.

I go to the next one and pull it out as well. By this time, I am not able to bring myself to go any further. It is not because I am scared or disgusted about periods, but what is so hard about wrapping up the discarded hygiene products? I did surgery on rats for the better part of two years in a neural-endocrinology laboratory, so blood does not bother me – in the right place. There is no need for the war crimes I witnessed that day.

I quickly mop the room and leave, heading to the store front and onto the other men's restroom. It is actually cleaner than the other, allowing me to move on quickly. At the woman's restroom, I again wait before being allowed access. This time, I am leaning against the wall between the two bathrooms for a good twenty minutes before I can enter. During this time, I notice a handful of cash registers not in use while customers are lined up four deep at each register that is being utilized. CSM Anna walks by and smiles at me, but she says nothing like, "Could you hop onto a register? We could use some help." No, she leaves me to do somebody else's job while mine is neglected.

Finally getting into the restroom, I find this one almost as bad as the other woman's restroom, but the mirror is not smeared, thankfully. I do not look at the receptacles in the stalls, preferring to leave it for maintenance tomorrow. Larry the bathroom guy should be here in the morning.

I finish the restrooms and put the cleaning supplies away only half an hour after my shift is over, though part of this time is the ten minutes I spend washing my hands.

I leave the store thinking I might not come back tomorrow, but I do come back, and am placed on a register the next day. My anger fades, though it is replaced with a different frustration.

12

Opening day was not a glorious day for any associate working on the floor, as little ran smoothly. Cashier Leah was running a register, checking out customers, and her line was long, and her customers impatient. She gradually became more frustrated as the day wore on, and a doughnut was the harbinger.

She had no idea how to ring up the doughnut. There was no bar code to scan, and she had never been shown how to use the PLU (Price Look Up) book placed at each register that contains codes for such items. Produce items are rung up in the same manner. Customer after customer kept coming with items she did not know how to handle, and the line only grew longer, adding more stress.

Then came the last straw. A carton of eggs came through, and she opened it to see if any eggs were broken, and her thumb punctured one, breaking the otherwise flawless egg. She stood there, looking at the broken egg, dumbfounded at what she just did. She looked at where her register's phone should have been to discover there was none. She looked to the cashier behind her, and then to the one before her. They both had phones but were too busy to help. Leah then realized she did not know who to even call for a new egg.

Leah sent a message to the CSM's palm pilots via her register saying she needed help. She waited. Leah sent another message, but to no avail. Finally fed up, she left her register and found CSM Kelly. "I need an egg," Leah said.

"Call someone," Kelly responded.

"I'm not calling anybody. Get me an egg now."

"No."

"God damn it! Get me an egg now."

"No," Kelly proclaimed again.

"Fine. I don't need this shit. I quit!"

"What?"

"I'm done with this. I don't need this job. I quit." Leah walked away from Kelly then. She passed by CSM Faye and said, "I quit. There is a line at my checkout, so somebody better go help them because I'm not."

She headed to the back of the store then, bawling. Managers saw her and began to follow. In the back, they asked what was wrong. Leah replied, through her crying, "I don't need this shit. I'm done."

They had her take a break to dry her eyes and blow her nose. She asked to come back the next day, but management talked her into staying to finish her shift by promising a shorter line with lighter loads. Leah stayed, which she says was a good thing, because she would not have come back the next day.

When Leah returned to the store's front, CSM Kelly apologized. Leah admits Kelly was stressed too. Nothing was working right for anyone, and Leah does not blame Kelly. This store

14

no longer checks egg cartons, but I do not believe that has anything to do with Leah.

# For Whom the Bell Dings

**By James**

I usually do not mind coming to work after being off four or five days. It is almost like I forget how much this place frustrates me. Today is like that, and I am feeling great. I clock in and head to the deli, where I find two of my co-workers. One of them will leave shortly, but I feel I can handle it today. I am ready to go, and it is go time!

The hot case is stocked perfectly, everything having been made within the last fifteen minutes. Rotisserie chickens have just finished cooking, and the fried chicken was done twenty minutes before. I grab a rag only to notice the tables are already clean, so I head to stir the salads, but my co-worker says it already has been done. The dishes are also caught up. There is literally nothing to do.

At this point, I say, "Then I guess I'll just pack up and go home. Good job ladies. You have a fine night."

They both smile at me, and my supervisor says, "I don't think so, little man. I'm leaving in two minutes, and Kim still has her lunch break."

As my supervisor departs, Kim, my other co-worker, asks, "What time do you want me to go to lunch?"

Having not been assigned the duty of babysitting her, I answer, "Whenever you feel like it." To most deli workers, this carries the inference they should go soon enough to be back before supper rush. Not Kim; I forgot she takes words at face value.

She says, "Sounds good. I'll go here in a bit."

"A bit" becomes almost an hour, during which we had two customers. At two minutes before five o'clock, she heads to lunch, leaving me alone during the busiest time of day. Sure enough, minutes after her departure, three people come to the meat case wanting sliced meats and cheeses while another approaches the hot case and rings the bell repeatedly, seemingly to inspire me to leave my present customers and ease her hunger.

I cut over ten pounds of meat and cheese before I can head to the hot case, but by then, the lady at the hot case has given up, inevitably cursing me on her way to another food supplier.

Cashier Deloris, who is leaving for the night, asks me to make a fresh eight piece chicken packet then. I tell her it will be ready in twenty-five minutes, and she agrees to come back. I look at the hot case to see if I need to fry any more chicken as well. There are five pieces, which usually last an hour.

I put the one eight piece chicken down and move to help someone at the meat case. I shave six pounds of meat while someone new practices playing the bell. By the time I get to this guy, he looks at me and starts to walk away. He says, "I was going to get a medium barbeque, but you took too long. I guess you can just deal with the loss." He walks off. Just like that, the deli is out three dollars. I figure we will find a way to make ends meet, somehow.

With fourteen minutes still remaining on the eight piece chicken, I hear the bell at the hot case ring again. A family of three requests an eight piece chicken, and as I attempt to show them where they are, I see the five eight pieces are gone though I never noticed anyone take even one. I apologize and tell them it will be about half an hour before more will be ready. He says he will come back just as the meat case bell rings.

This customer gives me the joy of shaving three pounds of ham, as well as cutting another pound and a half of cheese. Two more customers follow, and it is almost ten minutes before I can drop chicken into the fryer. I do not literally drop the chicken anymore, because that would be stupid as it sends hot grease flying

18

all over me every time. I only get the breasts down as the hot case bell dings. I am surprised to see the same family from before, and they ask if the chicken is ready. I inform them I am just dropping the eight pieces now.

"Well, you said half an hour."

"Yes, and that was ten minutes ago, but I've been busy, and I'm the only one back here. I haven't been able to...."

"Then you need to get more help back here."

"I agree."

The father suddenly becomes angry, and, in front of his five or six year old child, he yells, "Well, I'm not gonna wait around all day. Why don't you just fuck your chicken and see how you like that?" They leave.

I stare at the guy in complete disbelief. I do not see how engaging in intercourse with the poultry will make my job any easier. I brush it off and move on as the bell rings at the meat counter.

The lady there says, "I'm not really sure what I want yet. Can you give me a minute?"

I do not understand why she would call me over when she needed nothing. For wasting my precious time, I can envision walking around the counter, placing my hand on the back of her neck and calmly slamming her face into the counter until she makes up her mind. Knowing such a response would be a poor choice, I instead say, "Absolutely. I'm going to place more chicken in the fryer. I'll be right back."

"Alrighty then."

I put the thighs in the fryer and hear the bell again. I look, and that lady is the only one at the counter. I walk back over, leaving the rest of the chicken waiting. "Did you figure out what you want?"

"Yeah, give me the roast beef."

"Which one would you like?"

"Whichever." Not a good answer. We have many different types that vary in price, quality, and flavoring. I start explaining the differences to her so she better understands what we offer, but she interrupts to say, "I really don't care. Give me whatever."

I give her the regular roast beef, which is the cheapest of our selection. I ask how she wants it sliced, and she says, "Whatever you want." I am beginning to hate the word "whatever" at this point. I cut the meat, bag it, and put the price sticker on it. She says, "Good," and walks away. A "thank you" would have obviously been asking too much.

I return to the fryers and drop the drumsticks and wings and start the timer. The breasts and thighs will most likely be burnt when everything comes up, but I no longer care. My carefree attitude is gone, and I just want to go home. I look from the fryer in time to see my favorite family walking by and hear the dad say,

20

"See that shit?  They still don't have any chickens in there."

When Kim returns, I say to her, "In the time you have been gone, I have cut over twenty-two pounds of meat and cheese, remade half the hot case, and cooked an entire case of chicken pieces."

She smiles and says, "Good job.  See?  You don't need me."

I consider slamming her face into the hot case at this point.

# Associopaths I

**By James**

The break room at Wal-Mart can be a strange place, even for those here every day. I am on a fifteen minute break right now, my first of the day. Currently, eleven people are in the room, and I know all but two of them.

Tim from frozen is sitting alone, reading *Wal-Mart World*. This is Wal-Mart's internal magazine, which is filled with interviews of staff from stores across the world, each talking about how great Wal-Mart has been for their lives. All in all, the magazine offers a skewed look at how wonderful the company is, and how we all should appreciate the way Wal-Mart enriches our lives. Nobody really seems to enjoy the magazine. For fun, I make edit marks to correct the consistently horrible grammar, but only when I is really bored.

Darlene from pharmacy is talking about her wedding again. She got married a month ago, but she talks about it almost as much as before the event. Holly from menswear stares at Darlene while smiling, nodding her head, and looking like she really relishes the story. I have known Holly long enough to realize that, though listening, she wants Darlene to shut her mouth. Holly pays attention to the story only to find whatever gossip she can.

At Wal-Mart, people *live* for gossip. In fact, the only thing that travels faster than gossip is STD's -- and the two go hand in hand. Most everyone longs to know who is sleeping with whom, especially if one is cheating, and then they openly wonder how anyone could be so stupid while disregarding that they slept around. Considering the great ease of picking up co-workers, one might think Wal-Mart could find a way to profit from it -- other than the side effect of creating future employees and customers.

As I am typing, Lana from shoes sits nearby and interrupts me mid-thought. I do not mind when this happens, because the stories told in the break room are what keep me here inside rather than leaving for breaks. People say and do the most idiotic things on the sales floor, but it is easy to miss them in such a big store. In the break room, associates feel the incessant need to share the craziest things they see throughout the day.

Lana says, "I had the greatest phone call today."

"Judging by your tone, that's that 'sarcasm' thing I've been hearing about...."

Lana had been working in shoes when the intercom announced a phone call for her department. She picked it up and heard, "Hey, you got shoes?"

"Yeah...."

"Awesome. I need to get some."

"What kind, sir?"

"What?"

"What kind of shoes are you looking for? We sell several different types."

"Well...." He paused for about ten seconds before saying, "Well, I guess I would need some like the ones I'm wearing. They're very comfortable."

"What?"

"The ones I'm wearing. Do you have any?"

Lana shakes her head. "And that was it. When I tried to ask what he was wearing and explain that I couldn't see them, he got mad and hung up. Who would have thought that the customers at home are weirder than the ones in the store?"

I agree with Lana. One night in the deli, we received a phone call on line three. I picked up, saying, "Wal-Mart Deli. How can I help you?"

"Do you carry Pedigree?"

"I'm sorry?"

"In the green bag."

"In the green bag?"

"Yeah, Pedigree in a green bag."

"This is the deli."

"Yeah!"

"Ma'am, I think you must want the pet department."

"Well, yeah."

"This is the deli."

"That's where they sent me."

"Where?"

"To the deli. They said you could help me."

"They must not have understood. You need someone in the pet department."

"I know that. Transfer me."

"I can't."

"What do you mean you can't?"

"I really can't. My phone does not allow me to put you on hold and transfer you to a different department."

"Great. So I'm screwed then?"

"No, if you just hang up and call back, tell them to transfer you to the pet department. They should be able to help you."

"And how long will that be?"

"How long will what be, ma'am?"

"Until they're back."

"Who?"

"Huh?"

"Until who is back?"

"The people that can help me."

"They're here now. You just need to...."

"So can you transfer me over to them?"

"No."

"So I'm screwed?"

"No. They are here. I just need you to hang up, call right back, and ask to talk to someone in the pet department."

"And they'll help me?"

"They should."

"Well, all right. Thank you. Have a great night."

As I hung up, I could not decide if I was annoyed by the conversation or just happy that someone actually said "thank you" to me.

Lana heads back to shoes, leaving me and four others. I know them enough to realize they will not tell me any interesting stories, so I head back to the deli, hoping for a better group when I return for lunch.

On my way out of the break room, I overhear CSM Donna

talking. She was at the service desk when a customer came to the counter. The lady put a receipt in front of Donna, pointed to the last item on the list, and asked, "What does that say?"

Donna replied, "It says Bud Lite."

"And what is that?"

"Well... that's beer."

The lady blew up at that point, shouting, "I'll have you know I am a recovered alcoholic. I haven't drunk anything for over three years now. My cashier put this on my receipt. Why would she do that?"

Donna, coolheaded as always, looked at the receipt to see who the cashier had been. After seeing the operator number, Donna looked back at the lady and said, "You went through the self checkouts."

I hurry out of the room then before my laughter gives my eavesdropping away.

# If Interested, Get with Management

**By James**

There is a clear and simple reason why most companies have rules against dating co-workers. It usually is not a good idea -- yet it is impossible to completely avoid. Someone working forty hours a week spends nearly half of their waking hours at the workplace. It is ridiculous to think people spending such time together will not become attracted to one another. Companies have these rules about dating because it can, and often does, affect work, either while seeing each other, after breaking up, or both.

Wal-Mart dating rules do not actually bar associate dating, nor do they state that management and associates cannot date, which most would expect. Wal-Mart's policy is simply associates cannot date who they work under or over. For instance, a deli associate is not allowed to date the deli lead, the assistant manager over the deli, the co-managers, or the store manager. However, that associate could literally sleep with anyone else in the store -- and some have tried. Of course, many have broken the one rule as well.

Since we met, which was during my second interview at Wal-Mart, I had a thing for Kayla, the deli lead. As I worked under her, I was not going to bother hitting on Kayla, so was I ever surprised when she started flirting with me. Within an hour, we were in the meat cooler, making out like hormone-driven high school students for half an hour.

Kayla invited me to her house that night, and I was up for the invitation. But then I talked to Chris from produce. As it turned out, Kayla had a fiancé serving in Iraq. I was mad for about two minutes, until I realized I had not bothered asking if she was single. "Plus," I reasoned, "she's the one that came on to me." When I told her I no longer was interested in stopping by her house, Kayla asked what changed my mind.

"You have a fiancé."

"I told you that."

"No, you didn't."

"Well, you didn't seem to care whether I was seeing anyone

when we were in the cooler."

"I assumed you weren't, but point being, I'm not going to do this." I walked away without waiting for a rebuttal.

Before long, I heard Kayla was talking behind my back, saying I was extremely rude and annoying. Chris later told me I was the flavor of the week as Kayla had tried sleeping with half the associates on the north side of the store, including him.

Chris' relationship with Kayla was not as unscrupulous as mine would have been since he did not work under her, or even with her; however, management was concerned about their relationship. Management would not leave Chris alone, repeatedly calling him to the management office with questions about the relationship. Store Manager Chad knew exact times Chris' car was at Kayla's apartment, when he stayed over, and how often they went to lunch together. Chris finally became tired of the prodding and ended the relationship.

Kayla moved on once more, sleeping with at least three people from the deli, and three or more associates throughout the rest of the store. Apparently, the assistant manager over Kayla did not care about her breaking fraternization rules, because he reportedly slept with her at some point as well. And this was not the only time someone under this assistant manager was on top of him as he also "fraternized" with an associate in the bins of the old store.

30

One might think we all should have learned something from these exchanges, but a couple months afterward, I started seeing a cashier named Karra. We went on a couple dates before I realized there was no real connection between us. I tried to move on, but Karra stalked me for a while, giving me strange gifts, emailing me constantly, and starting several rumors.

When I heard there was a possibility she might transfer to my department, I talked with Assistant Manager Randy about my concerns of her causing problems. Randy laughed it off and said, "If you don't wanna face the consequences of your hookups, you shouldn't sleep with a cashier."

I informed him that I neither found that comment funny, nor liked his direct inference I was sleeping with cashiers, as that was none of his concern.

He did not apologize, but instead told me, "Deal with it. Everybody from Chad down knows." I went directly to Store Manager Chad at that point.

I walked in and said, "Chad, I need to talk to you, and I need to do it now." He had me pull up a chair, and I told him about my interaction with Randy.

He said that sometimes Randy is "a little rough around the edges but means well." We then dropped all talk of Randy and simply went into why I did not believe Karra should work in the deli. Apparently, he did not know. I explained the gifts and emails and rumors.

Chad said, "Ah, stalker type?"

"I suppose that's as good a term as any." I did not want to use those words myself.

Chad said, "I'll take care of it."

And that was it. If the roles had been reversed, with a male associate stalking a female associate, a bigger deal would have been made of the situation. Sexual harassment might have been voiced once or twice before it was all said and done.

True to his word, Karra was not allowed to come to the deli, but it upset me I had to defend my position because I am male. This one lesson, more than any other, taught me I should never date anyone at work again.

Kayla and I are, by far, not the only people who have dated co-workers. I know of at least fifteen other associates. For some, it led to long relationships, engagements, and even marriage. For others, sex was the only interest.

Support Manager Scott made it his own personal goal to -- in his words -- "sample everything Wal-Mart has to offer, and then some." Scott was notorious for sleeping with co-workers, most prominently a married woman named Holly. They tried to pretend nothing happened, and yet, they insisted on being together whenever possible, going to lunch together, and even playing footsie in the break room.

32

When Holly broke it off with Scott, he went around telling stories about her to anyone who would listen. He gave details of their sex life, such as the positions she liked best, and how close Holly's husband had come to catching them in bed together. She turned Scott in for sexual harassment after hearing of his stories, and upper management talked with him, but they did not do anything about it. Apparently, managers do not have to play by the rules. Management told Scott to start following the rules more closely and stop flirting with those under him.

Scott was rumored to have slept with as many as fourteen other associates. Unfortunately, I was not able to test the validity of this claim, as many of the girls left for college, while the others instantly became mad when Scott's name was mentioned.

Scott left Wal-Mart about the same time Kayla's engagement ended. Given the fact that they had each tried to sleep with almost everyone in the store, it was only a matter of time before they found one another. As of this writing, Scott and Kayla have been together for six months and are happily living together and now married. The next generation of management should be here in time for the New Year.

# You Know What
# Really Bugs Me...

**By R.A. Wilson**

The warm blowing air inside the front doors greets me, which I assume is supposed to be a reprieve from the heat outside. This strikes me as stupid.

At this point, if I could know how normal of a day I am about to have, I would go home instead. But I have no idea, so I walk to the back, already five minutes late. Being late seems endemic anymore, almost as if the idea of Wal-Mart being my destination makes it harder to leave home. Maybe I will not come anymore, but the bills always arrive the same time each month, almost like clockwork. They are getting quite predictable, really.

There are people walking around me, few noticing the "Enter" and "Exit" signs as traffic flows both ways through the doors. People Greeter Reuben smiles at me and says, "Good evening."

I wave back, thinking "good" is the wrong word for today. He should feel ashamed for offering such false hope. I am already grumpy at this point, but then a gentleman, seeming to want to make me feel better, rams me with his cart. I guess I should apologize for calling him a gentleman, because I would think a gentleman would not run into somebody and not even say "excuse me."

He does not make eye contact, but he probably feels high-and-mighty with that 32 inch LCD TV in his cart. I could say what is on my mind as I am not working yet, but that would make me even later. Reprimanding him would also have taken energy, and I prefer to spend as little energy in the store as I can. I walk around the man and hurry to the time clock. Behind me, the security system beeps as the man walks though, but Reuben waves him on while apologizing for the system acting up. He gets an apology even though he could not offer me one. A gentleman indeed.

Walking to the store's rear, I try to not look directly at anyone. For some reason, a few customers can sense I work here even when I am out of the blue smock. It is really annoying when someone asks if I work here when I am in street clothes. How does one answer that? Do I lie, only for her to find me in electronics minutes later wearing the blues? Or should I say yes, just not now? She would only get upset when I do not help her.

Not acknowledging people is the best way around this. I do not want to be any later. Besides, helping her would be working off the clock, and I can get written up for such action. It is illegal to make employees work of the clock, but Wal-Mart turns the law around so employees are at fault for any violation, even though the law is designed to protect the worker. This is all thanks to lawsuits the company has faced. Individuals make a lot of money by suing Wal-Mart, but they create a lot of hassle for the workers left behind.

I finally clock in and walk onto the floor. Becky is here, organizing the game case, making sure everything is put away properly and looking good. This is what we call zoning. She and I are the only ones who alphabetize the videogames, even though everyone is supposed to do so. Not even electronics' Department Manager Allison takes the time to do it. Usually, games are shoved into any open spot and left for Becky to fix later. We greet each other, and I give her a lame excuse for my tardiness. She hears these almost every day we work together. She just laughs and brushes it off.

"Who else is in today?" I ask.

"Allison opened, and Sheri is working the midshift with me.

You're closing?"

"Of course. What other time do I work?" I say. "So, what's going on today?"

"Directs have been worked already, and Sheri has been facing the CD's." Facing is similar to zoning in that it makes them look good by turning them all the right direction and keeping them uniform, but different in that it does not organize them better.

I lean up against the shelving across from her. "So, customer service and zoning?"

"Uh huh," she replies with a smile. In other words, it is going to be a boring night.

*1:18.* Just eight hours and forty-two minutes left minus lunch. The day is only starting.

"Have you seen Allison yet?" Becky asks.

I frown. "Why? Is she grumpy?" I really hate that, because Allison will make sure everyone is unhappy. She is good at ruining otherwise good days.

"Someone stole another TV yesterday."

And now I feel like a jerk because the frustration of such events weigh heavily on me as well. "When?"

"6:03 at night."

"I was on lunch. Joeltron was on the floor though." I thought, not my fault, but in all fairness, it is not Joel's fault either as there is little we can do to stop theft. "Joeltron" is Joel, but this mid-forties ex-Navy service man that appears to have lost his mind wants to change his last name to Tron, just to help him start over in life. So we call him Joeltron to help out.

"Well, there were two guys with two carts. One had a 32 inch Samsung LCD, and the other had a $658 computer, among other stuff. They walked out the TLE doors."

I do not ask how this happened as I already know. It might seem crazy that someone could merely leave the store with an unpaid TV and no one stops them, but the truth of the matter is it happens often. This particular time cost Wal-Mart twenty-one hundred dollars.

Since inventory almost five months ago, over seventeen-thousand dollars in just LCD's have walked out. That's more then what I made last year. And people say Wal-Mart does little for communities. The funny part is, Co-Manager Pete ordered a locking case, but corporate office cancelled the order because of expense. I am sure a locking case would have cost more than seventeen-thousand dollars. Way to go corporate!

I was amazed when the first TV walked out. How could anyone think that would work? The TV's have security tags, and surely someone watches for this. But then the second disappeared. The third. The tenth. After so many times, it seemed almost brilliant. Of twenty attempts, seventeen were successful.

The first theft attempt was stopped because the people

greeter did something amazing -- her job. The security sensors went off as usual, and the thief tried to keep walking like nothing happened, as they all do. People Greeter Arlene scooted over to him and said, "Excuse me, sir?"

He stopped. "Yes?"

"Can I see your receipt for that TV?"

"My wife has it. She already went to the car."

"Would you get the receipt then?"

"Um, I actually haven't paid for it yet. My wife has the checkbook, and I have to get it from her."

"Then you need to leave the TV here with me."

He left and never came back for the TV. Arlene received kudos for stopping the theft, which is a randomly chosen forty-eight cent candy bar. Something still seems wrong to me. She stopped a $400 TV theft, and in return she gets a forty-eight cent candy bar. Good job Arlene.

Normally, I would say she was doing her job and does not deserve a reward, but abnormal is normal here. She went well beyond her job, or at least she must have, because none of the other people greeters have done the same. Arlene deserves a bonus for her work. It just might prompt others to make attempts to stop theft instead of ignoring it. On the other hand, people greeters tend to be elderly or disabled people who can easily be intimidated by criminal elements. Also, theft does not affect them directly. Fundamental problems exist here.

The guy Arlene stopped is well known to the store because he has stolen numerous times. There are three other TV's he stole we know about, as well as a number of other items. My favorite story about this man was when he entered the store, walked to electronics, grabbed a $149 DVD burner, and took it to customer service and returned it. No door tag. No receipt. Sure, the money was put on a gift card that had to be spent in the store, but not too shabby for two minutes of work. He is not the only one to do this, and with no security, we are not able to check security cameras fast enough to know until the thieves are gone. This is why electronics is number one in loss merchandise, companywide.

One might wonder if the store knows who this guy is, why is he allowed in the store? I think it is lack of caring mostly. We have no security because corporate says we are not in need until holiday season, making no one responsible. One could argue management should take responsibility, but they are busy with their own jobs. By the time management can check the cameras, the thief will be gone.

It seems that keeping the customer happy is more important than catching a thief, even though each theft lowers store profit. This might not seem horrible, as our store breaks one and a half million a year in profit, but the year-end bonus given to associates is affected greatly. It only takes a shift of ten thousand dollars of store profit to affect hundreds of dollars given to each associate. The theft hurts associates but is negligible to corporate, so why would they care?

Management used a similar philosophy last holiday season. The game case is always locked, but when the department became busy, we could not keep up with the customers, prompting some to leave empty handed. Management opened the game case to allow customers free access, arguing any theft would be offset by higher sales. Perhaps. One fifty dollar game is not much of a loss, but twenty or so are. We were allowed to lock one case, but only after someone tried to steal the X-Box 360 demo unit the year it was released.

*1:21.* Eight hours and thirty nine minutes left, minus the one hour lunch.

Becky and I chatter a little longer until I see Allison, which prompts me to walk the department to look like I am doing something worthwhile. Allison leaves about an hour and a half later, and Becky and Sheri come and go to their lunch breaks. Five o'clock rolls around and I head to lunch with nothing noteworthy happening.

*6:03.* I clock back in. Becky is on the sales floor alone as Sheri left early. An hour later, Becky leaves, and I am by myself for the busiest time of the day, like usual. This is the time when I have three phone calls and six customers demanding my attention

41

simultaneously. My last three hours tend to go faster, albeit more stressful. God forbid management answer one of the phone calls as they know I am alone and cannot talk to three different phone lines at once.

*7:27.* Two hours and thirty-three minutes left.

Associate Larry the bathroom guy walks over to me with an armful of items. "Here you go." He places them on my counter.

"What's this?" I dig through the items. Two graphing calculators cut from their packaging, and an unopened electric toothbrush.

"I found these in the woman's restroom, sitting on the back of the toilet. Someone cut them open, but it looks like they got scared and gave up."

He is probably right. Packaging from stolen items is often found in restrooms. Security tags are rarely on items, so removing them from the packaging alleviates that problem for the thief. CD's and DVD's are stolen the same way, but they usually are not taken into bathrooms. They are opened with razorblades or knives while on the sales floor, and the disks are taken, leaving cases behind. I find handfuls of empty cases all the time.

I find even more since corporate announced they are not prosecuting shoplifting under twenty-five dollars. The store's theft log shows a fourfold increase since then. In the weekend after this announcement, we lost over five hundred dollars of CD's alone.

42

Corporate chose this policy to shift focus from customer theft to associate theft. In other words, a non-employee can steal that newest DVD and not have to worry about prosecution, even if caught, but if I steal a thirty-three cent pack of gum, I will go to jail. It is nice to be trusted.

I repackage the calculators and place them back on the shelf. As for the electric toothbrush, it goes to the return carts. I check my watch again.

*7:48.* Almost down to two hours now.

A customer approaches me and asks for a Playstation Portable, or PSP, to be taken to customer service for an exchange. I grab one from the case and walk up front. If I knew what I would find waiting, I might have been slightly more prepared. This customer, and his family, are returning a PSP bought earlier today, claiming the screen cracked. I almost laugh when I look the system over. It is absurd.

First off, for those who don't know, the PSP is one of the most powerful portable gaming systems ever made, but it was not created with children in mind. That said, it is easily damaged, even if well cared for with screen protectors and hard cases. The one they wish to return is scratched horribly. The screen looks like they tried to wipe it clean with a rock, and not just once. The plastic casing is chipped, much like it was thrown on a hard surface numerous times; perhaps their screen cleaning rock. The unit is also just plain dirty from use. The screen is shattered like they said but is only visible when turned on.

The serial number on the receipt matches the box and sticker on the unit, and the date and time shows they did indeed buy it earlier today. What I notice as I check the serial number on the PSP is the sticker is curled up on both ends. I pull lightly on it, and it comes off. This sticker is designed to not be removable, lest it be changed from unit to unit, allowing someone to return an older unit under the pretense of being a newer one, which is exactly what these people are trying to do.

This is what I want to say.

"You're joking, I hope."

"About what?" the customer's mom would ask, angry.

"This PSP obviously has been mistreated. I will not return it."

"We bought it today, and it was like this in the box. Maybe you should check them before accepting returns."

"This was a returned unit?"

"I bet it was."

"Well, we do check each unit to verify the serial numbers, and we look them over before putting them back on the shelf. I'm sorry, but no."

If this was the conversation I had, management would have been called, and we would have replaced the PSP and given the customer a gift card for the "inconvenience." I, no doubt, would have ended up in the management office afterward being lectured on proper ways to treat customers.

This is the conversation I actually had.

"You bought this one today?"

"Yes."

I keep my eyes on the PSP and say, "Okay."

That is it. I allow the return of a unit that is not returnable. I have little choice, and I really want to argue with her, but I still need this job. Those pesky bills again. I am not going to allow someone attempting to steal from Wal-Mart to make me unable to pay my mortgage.

Associates are constantly hearing from management that we need to take more responsibility upon ourselves. They say we are supposed to act like this is our Wal-Mart. The problem is that we are not empowered to do so. If my fear of being dragged to management is justifiable or not, the fact that I am worried at all shows we are not empowered as such.

Customer service is actually where a great deal of theft happens, and we do it to ourselves. People buy new items and return old ones in the new box, much like the PSP. Others place less expensive items in a more expensive item's box. For instance, a customer buys two calculators, one for a hundred dollars and the other for one-hundred fifty dollars. The less expensive calculator is stuffed into the one-hundred fifty dollar's box. It is returned, letting the customer keep the more expensive calculator for fifty dollars off. If they do this twice, they actually get a calculator for free.

Another time, a customer bought a DVD player at a self checkout, took it out of the box and put it in a bag. He took the bag to his car and brought the empty box back. He walked to electronics, placed the box on the shelf and took a full one. At customer service, he returned it with the receipt, getting his DVD player for free.

What annoys me the most is when a customer buys a TV and brings it back later, wanting to exchange it. Wanting a different TV is not a problem in itself, but the condition of the returned TV is. Screens can be scratched and casings scuffed, but one particular return was absurd. The casing was cracked open, and the screen broken. On its top was a discolored scuff that obviously was the point of impact that damaged the TV. They brought it back, claiming it was in the box as such. I might have believed that if the box was damaged, but since it was not, that would mean the TV came from the factory in such shape. Quality control would notice that kind of damage. This is what actually happened: when the TV was set wherever it was to stay, it fell, hitting something hard and breaking. Of course, management okayed the exchange. The customer destroyed their TV, and we replaced it for them.

*8:23.* I am in a horrible mood now. I talk with Assistant Manager Ron and Store Manager Chad about the PSP. They think it unfortunate but feel nothing could have been done. This makes no sense to me. Nothing can be done to protect us? We cannot reject a return that Sony will? All defective items are returned to the manufacturer, and they repay us if the unit is refundable. Sony, I am sure, saw this unit as nonrefundable.

Rarely, items are brought back that I can deny. This is typically software, DVD's, CD's, portable DVD players, digital audio players, computers, and big screen TV's. Federal copywrite law keeps us from returning the software (which includes videogames), CD's, and DVD's once opened. How are we to know they have not made copies? Sure, we can exchange them for the exact same thing if defective, but we can do nothing else. Only the copywrite holder can refund money.

And then some customers try to claim being offended by the content. Since these high moral customers do not want their child playing a game with violence and hookers, they need to check the ESRB rating. Grand Theft Auto is rated M for a reason, and the rating is printed on the videogame's front. The problem here is that it requires the customer to read.

*9:12.* Less than an hour to go.

I am now looking at every customer and thinking "What are you trying to steal?" It is hard to not glare at people when you feel like this. I think to myself that I could use a distraction, and as I walk toward the DVD's, a customer calls to me from behind. I turn around and walk to him.

"Can you tell me about the Toshiba laptops?" he asks.

"Sure." I smile, believing this will distract me from my frustration.

"Are they good, or crap?"

"Toshiba Satellites? They're excellent computers."

"Are they better then the Compaq?"

"Yeah. HP owns Compaq, and though HP is a good brand, Compaq tends to be their lower end models. Toshiba Satellites are not quite as good as Sony Vaio's, but they are close."

"Are these Wi-Fi enabled?"

"Wireless internet? As far as I know, all laptops are wireless now. Every one we carry is."

He asks me a few more questions, but I begin to realize he is not listening all that much. And then from behind me comes one of his friends, from where I had been walking when he first called me over. They walk away now, his last question unanswered, leaving me to stare at them in disbelief. He was distracting me while his friend stole something.

That is not the distraction I intended.

*9:41.* The day is pretty much done.

As I get ready to leave for the night, I notice the Tracfones are gone. There were sixty some phones earlier. Good sales, one might think, but when they disappear so quickly, it only means one thing.

This has happened twice before, and it again shows the brilliance of criminals. The phones themselves run under twenty dollars, but they are much more expensive to produce. The Tracfone company makes the money back on the phone service one must buy to use the phone, but these people are not buying the phones to use them as they are meant to be used. The first thing to do is page management. Assistant Manager Shaun calls, and I inform her that the phones are gone so management can do whatever it is management does. I call CSM Kris as well, who then calls the garden center to make sure all the doors are watched.

The first time this happened, Joeltron sold seventy-two Tracfones to two customers who claimed they were for a summer camp. When Joel rang up the fourth phone, the cash register denied the sale, saying it was a restricted item, allowing only three sold per customer per day.

Joeltron paged management, and Assistant Manager Jen replied. She said to go ahead and sell the phones. They were sold, three per transaction because of the restriction, and the two men left the store. Next day, the store was called by the police department and told the packaging was found from seventy-two Tracfones in a dumpster, the phones and batteries gone. At that time, management was told they were probably using the lithium from the batteries to make methamphetamines.

Allison called other stores in the area to let them know about this, but she found they too had been hit. Not even two weeks later, it happened again, but this time the two men were smarter. They then knew the phones were a restricted item, so they placed a spacer between every three. The cashier never rang up the fourth to know they were restricted. The two men came in at night, and the night crew was not informed about the scam. They made off with some fifty phones, showing the poor communication within the store.

Now, they are trying it again. I figure management will comb the store looking for the men with the phones, but not even two minutes later I see members of management pulling pallets onto the floor.

I approach Assistant Manager Silvia and say, "My Tracfones are all gone."

"I noticed that about half an hour ago."

"I just noticed about five minutes ago."

"A lot of people must be buying them today," she says.

How was I to respond to that? "This is the third time this has happened." She does not seem to understand what I am talking about. "They are buying the phones to make methamphetamines."

"No," she says. "The police told us that is not what's happening."

Apparently she does know. "Then what are they doing?"

50

"It's not for us to know."

"What?"

"That's what the police said." She walks off, pulling her pallet.

I am flabbergasted. What else would they be using the phones for? Who buys hundreds of cellular phones each day? It cannot be something legal, but she does not seem to care.

I think I understand. Management might have been told it was not to make methamphetamines, and they chose to believe this. They let sales go through to increase profit while not having to wonder how many people will use the drugs and possibly die. I know management is not all that bad, but this is selective ignorance.

I find out later that management was told something from the police, but they decided to not share it with us. Apparently, these people are buying the phones to sell them on the black market in Europe for two-hundred dollars a pop. My first question is: why do they throw away the packaging and battery charger? My second question is: If the phones barely work around this area, why would they work in Europe? They would not have the right SIM card. And finally: Why are the Europeans not just buying them from the website directly and saving one-hundred eighty dollars?

Two weeks later I read the real story about the phones on CNN.com. Terrorists. I'm not joking. Terrorists were trying to destroy the Mackinac Bridge in Michigan and were using Tracfones because they are untraceable. They had in their possession about one-thousand phones bought in the Midwest. They do not buy service but instead use the ten minutes they come with, so no particular phone is used more than once. And as the phones come with a small charge on the battery, the charger is not needed. Again, brilliant.

*10:07.* I finally clock out for the night, but this day will haunt me for a while. Even before I leave, Connie from domestics says to me, "There was a group of guys tonight that bought a bunch of Tracfones. They are selling them on EBay."

"Who told you that?" I ask.

"A cashier."

"That's not what they are using them for."

Cashier Katrina approaches us then. "Yeah, I sold some to one guy, and then a little later, another came through my line."

I ask, "They bought them in transactions of three, right?"

"Yes. How did you know?"

Again, the lack of communication shows. The cashiers that end up selling the phones have not been informed. "They are restricted items. They buy them in groups of three so the computer doesn't prompt you."

"Is that why they put those restricted item stickers at the registers? I thought that was to remind us that products containing suphedrine couldn't be sold more than three at a time."

"No, that was for the Tracfones."

"They said nothing about Tracfones."

I no longer feel like talking, my frustration high enough to make me incoherent. I leave the store and drive home, all the while thinking: "I need a new job."

# Walking Out One Night

**By James**

I hate walking into this place.  Sometimes, though, walking out can actually be worse.  I clock out and grab my backpack, which holds my homework and laptop.  I walk past two members of management standing in electronics, and they both glare at me, watching as I pass the CD rack.  I smile and keep going, deciding since I am off the clock, there is no reason to let them talk at me.  I walk to the DVD rack and grab the movie I have been thinking about buying-- *Goodfellas*.

Working for Wal-Mart is a lot like *Goodfellas*.  The film is about low totem pole Mafia men trying to work up the ladder even though they know they cannot reach the top. Ultimately, they take the fall while the Mafia moves on without caring they were ever there. I notice this irony and laugh as I look at the two "made men" still watching me from earlier.

I walk to a cash register and pay for the movie before stopping at the deli to talk with my coworkers. Courtesy Associate Darold approaches the deli counter and leans down to my ear, saying, "Hey, I just thought you'd like to know that there was some guy with a backpack stealing some CD's, and management is looking for him. I was going to point out that you had a backpack just so I could tackle you, but I decided to let you know instead." He laughs and then heads outside, telling me to have a good night.

I become paranoid as I approach the security devices at the front doors. I know I have not stolen anything, but the thought has been planted that something bad is about to happen. I can see myself walking through the electronic surveillance system, and it beeps because the cashier did not deactivate my DVD. Then management descends upon me as Darold tackles me into the wall. They would go through all my homework and check files on my laptop before deciding I did not have a receipt for my computer and send me to Wal-Mart jail.

I know there is no Wal-Mart jail, at least to my knowledge, and I realize the machine will not beep at me. Even if it does, the people greeter will probably just wave me through. Still, I am relieved when I make it through without the alarm going off.

Once outside, I see Darold again. He is pushing carts, which seems to be the only thing people think courtesy associates do. This simply is not the case; in fact, the courtesy associates should have their official title changed to Wal-Mart Bitches. It would be more accurate and display the lack of respect they receive. Courtesy associates are expected to do anything they are told to do at any time, by any manager, associate, and customer.

Darold parks the carts and approaches me. "So, tonight this guy bought this television and tells me that he needs some help taking it to his truck. I said, 'No problem, bro.'"

"So we get the TV out the doors, and he points to this Mac truck parked over by Arby's. In my head, I'm like, 'That's two football fields away.' But I smiled. I thought maybe he was just yanking my chain, but no, this guy was serious. So I haul this 32 inch TV all the way down there, and he opens up the cab of the truck. He wants to put this TV in the sleeper of the cab! Can you believe that? So I figure I'll give it a shot. He climbs up in the cab and wants me to hoist it up to him. I hand it up to him, and he tries to pull it into the truck, but we get stuck on the armrest and the steering wheel. So he pushes it back down to me, lopsided. I hoist it back up to him and the same thing happens again. Finally, he gets it in there, and then I climb up, and we push the thing into the sleeper. He looks at me and says, 'All right, then.' Not 'thank you,' or 'that sucked,' or anything. Just 'all right then.' Can you believe that?"

I said the only thing I could: "That sucks."

"Yeah. Earlier, I got called to three registers within two minutes of each other. Every time, they ask for me personally. None of the other courtesy guys are doing shit, unless you count Doug playing with himself over there, but nothing important." Darold points to the south, making me wonder. "But they want me. They had to use Doug, because I couldn't help everyone at once. Then, when I'm coming back in, that cashier, what's her name? Megan? She glares at me because Doug apparently almost dropped the carryout. What is wrong with people, man? I can't do every carryout."

"That's messed up."

"Oh, and Chad yelled at me again last night."

"Store Manager Chad?"

"Yeah. He comes over the walkie-talkie and says he needs a courtesy guy back at layaway to help him with a carryout for another television. I said I'd be right there. I'm on my way back there, by electronics, and a customer stops me and asks where the stuffed crab claws are. I stared at the idiot and said, 'Check seafood.'"

"Why do they do...?"

"So I get to the back, and Chad and the television are gone."

57

Darold talked through my unfinished question. "They're just gone. I see Sylvia, so I asked her where Chad was. She said, 'He's up by the GM doors, taking that TV out. I thought you were gonna help him.' I thought, 'So did I.' "

"I make my way up to the doors, and Chad's already outside, trying desperately to get the thing into the guy's van. I asked if he wanted help, and he said, 'I got it,' in kind of a 'go fuck yourself' tone. I had no clue what I had done wrong. When the customer left, Chad starts ripping me out, asking me where the hell I was. I tried to explain that I was going to layaway to meet him there, but he said that he had radioed for me to meet him up front. I told him I hadn't heard the message, and he said I need to start paying better attention to my radio. Then he just walks away before I could say anything else. I hate that dude sometimes."

Darold's walkie-talkie sounded, and he was off to the registers for a carryout. As he passed through the front doors, he turned and said, "Hey, you have a great night. Sorry I almost tackled you."

"It happens."

Darold has not been on friendly terms with Chad since he was told to not talk with people greeters anymore. Chad hinted Darold was partially to blame for stolen merchandise by distracting people greeters from doing their jobs. In reality, it is good to have Darold there at times.

One day, I saw people greeter AJ standing with his hands behind his back, gently rocking back and forth, looking like he was about to fall asleep. Perhaps he would have if Darold was not keeping him awake with chatter. AJ's face then suddenly came to life as a man entered the store with a hunting rifle, apparently trying to return it. He must have figured putting the gun in its box like a normal person would have been too much work. Darold ripped the rifle out of the man's hand, saying, "Give me that."

The man was stunned as he had no idea why his rifle was taken away. Darold explained Wal-Mart's policy to not allow customers to carry weaponry in the store; being Darold, that is not quite how he said it though.

Darold handed the rifle to AJ, who led the man to customer service. If Darold was not there, odds are AJ would have stuck a little pink sticker on the rifle and sent the man to customer service on his own, *if* that was where he was *really* going.

Darold had looked at me as the two walked away and said, "You know the most screwed up part of this?"

I said, "The guy with the gun?"

"No, the fact that somehow, they'll find a way to yell at me for this." He went back outside.

I never heard if Darold was reprimanded for the incident, but management did not applaud his actions either. He did not even get kudos for his efforts. It is Wal-Mart's way of thanking associates for going above and beyond their expected duties. Apparently, stopping a man with a gun is just one more duty expected of a courtesy associate.

# Associopaths II

**By James**

As I walk into the break room for my lunch, I see two people greeters, five floor associates, and three members of management. My own boss, deli lead Kathleen, is reading a book. While I understand the desire to escape Wal-Mart as a whole, I do not understand trying to escape the reality of the break room. The stories here alone make it worth my time to catch up with my co-workers. I know the people here today will be well worth talking with.

Two of the managers, Randy and Travis, are discussing the past weekend football games. Travis says, "The Huskers may have lost, but they are the first team to hold USC under thirty points in twenty-six games." I have no idea if that is true since I do not watch college football.

I sit down and pull out my laptop. Before I can even turn it on, Chris from produce walks in. "You *have* to put this in your book. You're never gonna believe what happened to me just now." I look toward the managers to see if they heard talk about a book, but they show no reaction.

Chris was in the bathroom wearing his blue Wal-Mart vest, standing at a urinal. A man slammed open the door and scanned the bathroom. He looked at Chris and said, "Where the fuck are they?"

Chris zipped his pants up and said, "Where are who?"

"The bottles."

"What bottles?"

"I left my baby bottles in here. Where the fuck are they?"

Chris looked at the guy as he tucked in his shirt and said, "I have no idea."

"Well, you work here, don't you?"

"I work in produce, not the bathroom."

"No shit."

"I can look around for you, but I don't know where they are."

"Well, that's just fucking wonderful. Where you gonna

look? Produce?"

Chris was confused at this point, but he tried to maintain his temper. "Sir, I would check the layaway counter, and if they're not there, I'll check customer service, because that's where...."

"How about you don't even worry about it?"

"Well, sir, if you want me to...."

"No. Fuck it. And fuck you too. My kid is just gonna go hungry without them. I hope you're happy." And then the man left.

Chris was slightly disturbed by this, but he let it go and went about his business. Five minutes or so went by when Chris realized his name tag was missing, so he retraced his steps, which eventually led back to the bathroom. While he was in there, the man returned.

"I know you fucking got 'em. Give 'em to me."

"Sir, I do not have your...."

The man pushed up against Chris. Chris stands 6'4", almost seven inches taller than this man. He was not scared as much as amazed this man was so aggressively stupid.

"I know you got my fucking bottles. Where the fuck are they?"

Chris stepped back. "Sir, I don't have your...."

The man screamed, "Gimme my goddamn bottles."

"Sir, I don't have them. I don't know if you think I just sit in the bathroom throughout my shift swigging on baby formula or some shit, but I don't."

"Don't get smart with me."

Chris tried to leave, but the man stepped in front of him.

"Sir, you need to drop this."

"I'll fucking drop you."

Chris said, "Try," and proceeded to walk past him and out the door.

After Chris tells me this, I say, "That's amazing. What would you have done if he had actually tried anything?"

"Taken my vest off and strangled his hick ass with it."

Another associate pipes up, "That's a customer. You can't do that."

Assistant Manager Randy says, "Why? I would. If he throws the first punch, I think you're on your own to do what you want." He pauses and smiles at Chris, "Plus, it's not like they have cameras in the bathroom." Randy is about as tall as Chris and resembles Mr. Clean. Randy was a professional boxer for years, and he is a bouncer for the strip joint uptown.

Chris says, "Well, I better get back up front before my boss realizes I'm not up there." He looks at Travis. "Right, Travis?"

His boss smirks. "Chris, you're never up front. I'm pretty used to it."

Chris pulls out a chair, "Well then...."

Travis looks at him and says, "Get up there." Chris waves

goodbye and leaves.

I start typing the story, and I hear Randy and Travis go back to their sports talk. They are trying to figure out the name of a player, so I turn on my Wi-Fi connection and search for it. I tell them his name, and they look at me perplexed. Randy says, "You have internet in here?"

"Yeah. It's Wi-Fi."

"How'd you get it?"

"Well, there's a wireless card in my laptop," I say, sounding like a smart ass. "I can hop on other people's internet connections with it."

"So you hacked into the Wal-Mart computer system?"

"What? No. Not at all. There's a house in the neighborhood around here with a wireless connection that I'm using."

"How? That's too far away."

"Well, it's a weak signal, but I can still...."

"So you didn't hack into the Wal-Mart system?"

"No. Why would I want to do that anyway?"

"You know, we can go on the system and find out if you were using it or not."

This is a bluff. If they do not even understand how Wi-Fi works, they will not be able to figure out if I'm using the store network or not. It does not matter anyway as Wal-Mart's wireless connection is encrypted. Besides, their network is not connected to the internet; it uses the Wal-Mart Wire instead.

I simply respond, "Well, go ahead. I'm not using it, so I won't show up, but if you wanna waste your time like that, feel free." I smile and go back to typing. They seem satisfied and return to their football talk. I receive no thank you for my trouble, but I am pretty used to that around here.

I look up after several minutes and see Assistant Manager Russ playing video games on his PDA. I laugh to myself, because I know he is playing a game he calls "Drug Smugglers." He really gets involved with the game, and that cracks me up.

Chris comes back in then, actually on break now. Randy and Travis get up to leave as Chris sits by me. Travis says as he walks out, "Don't be hacking into the system and giving Chris a raise."

Chris seems confused but does not comment on it, mostly because he has something else on mind. "What's this I hear you're gonna shoot a cow?"

"I'm not going to shoot a cow. Support Manager Aaron wanted to shoot the cow."

"Why?"

The whole thing started when I was helping the meat department today. I saw a customer staring at a package of T-bones; in fact, his nose was only four inches away from the packaging. I approached him and asked, "Can I help you with anything, sir?"

"Yeah. I need you to re-cut these steaks. You see all that fat on the meat? I want it trimmed off."

"We don't cut the meat here."

"Well how the hell do you get it then?"

"All of our meats are prepared at the meat packing plants. We simply take them out of the box and put them on the shelves."

"I just need the fat trimmed off a bit. I really don't want to pay for a bunch of fat that I'm not going to use."

"I can appreciate that, but I don't have anything to cut it with."

"Use a butcher's knife."

"I don't have a butcher's knife."

"Well, use some scissors."

"I don't have scissors either."

The man was becoming visibly upset. "Well then, just what the fuck do you cut stuff with back there?"

I pulled out my box cutter and showed it to him. He was not impressed.

"You think you're funny, kid?"

"I wasn't trying to be funny. This is seriously all I have."

"Well, what the fuck would you do if a cow walked in here?" That was what he said. Just like that. *What the fuck would you do if a cow walked in here?*

I didn't mean to respond like I did. It just came out. "I suppose I would take her to the pet department."

The man was now pissed.

"I want a manager over here, now."

I went and paged for management. As I did, I thought about what I would really do if a cow walked into my department. I jokingly thought I would simply page, "Would the owner of the big brown cow please come to the meat department? Your party is waiting." Then I realized that I would probably just run away and call for management when I got to wherever I ended up.

He saw me smiling as I went back to him, and he became even more upset. It seemed that my happiness was unpleasant to him. "Something funny, kid?"

"I was just picturing what I would do if a cow really did walk in here."

"Whatever. Where the fuck is your manager?"

I saw Support Manager Aaron walking over, so I pointed to him. "He's right there, sir. He'll be here any second."

The man proceeded to relay the entire conversation to Aaron, including what I said about taking the cow to the pet department. Aaron is a simple boy not quite twenty years old, so I was not overly surprised when he replied, "I don't think that would work. There's nothing big enough there to hold a cow."

The infuriated man walked away -- with his steaks. Aaron

looked at me and said, "You know what I would do? I'd call for a code nine (gun sale), a code brown (a shooting), and clean up in aisle seven." He smiled and walked away.

As I finish my story, Chris is laughing hysterically, and Assistant Manager Russ stares at me in disbelief.

Russ says, "I've been here for over twenty years, and I've seen some weird shit. And you know what? I have no idea what I'd do if a cow walked into the store."

Russ is not lying when he says he's seen some weird occurrences in Wal-Mart. One of the weirdest has to be the time he refused service to a customer. That, in itself, seems completely out of place at a Wal-Mart, but this particular case was well warranted. The guy was trying to buy rope, duct tape, and a knife. It made Russ uncomfortable, prompting him to deny the sale. As Russ puts it, "If I accomplished nothing else in my twenty years here, I feel I did the right thing that night."

A month later, the same person visited the Hy-Vee grocery store in town, and he grabbed the tie of a young teenage girl manning one of their registers. He pulled her toward him and cupped her breast, trying to rub her nipple through the shirt. He was, of course, instantly escorted out of Hy-Vee, and their management called the police, who in turn called our store so we could protect our associates.

When the girl left work, she came to Wal-Mart, and the man

followed her into the store. He stalked her through the aisles, making lewd comments, and his eyes never left her. Management called the police, who quickly came, thinking he was going to try abducting her. He was escorted out, this time by the police, and told to not come back. The police made sure he left the parking lot, and the girl reached home safely.

I look at the clock and see an hour has passed. Though I have to go back to work, I feel completely at ease. Somehow, the stories told in the break room make me feel better by helping me realize I am not the only one experiencing really strange stuff. It almost seems completely normal.

# Postwalmartem

**By R.A. Wilson**

There is a fairly universal truth throughout Wal-Mart, and it might seem shocking at first, especially when considering that nobody seems to acknowledge it. That is: whenever someone either quits or is fired suddenly, that person experiences a mental breakdown. About an hour or so before leaving the company, the person's behavior becomes erratic and completely out of character.

It is my opinion that this is the ultimate effect of having one's soul devoured. This company is not an evil entity, and I really do believe this, but its effect on the individual is detrimental. The total lack of respect and understanding destroys one's sense of self, making the individual a mindless drone treated as store property. It is degrading, but this is how the store runs.

There are three ways to deal with this phenomenon: become resistant, give in, or fall asunder. Lifers are those that give in. It is shocking to notice their personalities, because they behave like machines for the most part, moving from one repetitive task to the next. These people have developed multiple personalities: the Wal-Mart one and the real one. In this way, they have acquiesced to management, but have also found a way to keep their individuality intact.

There are those that resist, and those that fall apart. Dave is my personal hero because he resisted to the very end. He worked in sporting goods part-time as a second job. His Wal-Mart schedule needed to work around his other job, and this would include not just available hours, but days he could and could not work. He tried to coordinate days off for activities outside of work. His primary job was almost always agreeable, but Wal-Mart was another matter.

To get time off, one simply needs to put requested dates in the computer, and it will show up when management makes the schedule. Dave did as he was supposed to, even going as far as telling Assistant Manager Craig, who wrote his schedule, which days he needed off. In his last month with Wal-Mart, Dave was ultimately scheduled every day he asked off, including his vacation.

He talked to Craig about it, who replied that Dave should

have entered the days into the computer. Dave said he had, and Craig only apologized, leaving Dave to cancel his plans. It happened twice more that month. Oddly enough, it was when he did not get time off for a local softball tournament that pushed him too far.

Again he went to management. He found Wade and Pete, since Craig was on vacation. Dave told them his problem, Wade told Dave he had to be flexible for fairness to everyone. Dave removed his vest, put it in Craig's mailbox in the management office, and left a letter of resignation. This, again, is resistance. However, Dave is coming back, so management must be gearing up to take another jab at his defenses.

Then there are the others, those that fall apart, becoming only remnants of their personalities. These people have sudden changes in behavior so extreme, it could be termed personality inversion. Bob from receiving is a perfect example. He was a nice guy, always willing to lend a hand wherever and whenever one was needed, and he never had a bad word to say about anyone. But one day, everybody became Nazis.

Bob's job was to unload trucks and take the freight to the floor. Receiving uses a conveyer belt when unloading trucks to move freight into the receiving dock. As the boxes come out, others in receiving stack them on pallets to take to the floor at night.

There are three main doors that trailers back up to, all located on the same wall, close to each other. There is a table along this wall that holds a water cooler, a store phone, personal items, and a radio. It was the radio that pushed Bob over the edge.

When Travis works in receiving, he likes to tune the radio to country stations. Travis does this every day, and Bob dealt with it for more than a year, never saying a word about it. About an hour before he quit, Bob finally said something. He screamed, "Do we always have to listen to country? What are we, a bunch of Nazis?" Apparently, as American as country music is, Nazis are big fans. This went on for an hour, the music kept playing and Bob kept yelling.

The lead in receiving, Al, told Bob to take a break as he was starting to scare everyone with his erratic and uncharacteristic behavior. Bob left, and Al followed. Al asked Bob if he wanted to talk about anything, but Bob merely responded, "Fuck you."

Bob walked out without another word spoken. Al seemed distraught for a while after this, but he was able to talk with Bob some days later, though I have not seen Bob since. Poor Bob. I liked him, even when I heard that he had been eating rotisserie chicken from the garbage.

Eric the customer courtesy associate displayed the most radical inversion I have witnessed. Shortly after the store's first winter, the parking lot lights were to be sandblasted, and carts were placed upside-down in the parking spots adjacent to the light poles. Some people actually moved the carts to park in these spots.

When the sandblasting began, one car was in the way, so

Eric went inside the store and asked CSM Mary to page the customer to move their car. Eric had the license plate number for her, but Mary refused, saying customers can park where they like. Mary and Eric have had arguments in the past, but this was simply the last straw for Eric. It was bad timing too, because Eric was going to let me borrow the original Star Wars Trilogy, but because he got fired, that never happened.

Mary was standing behind the CSM podium, and Eric in front of it. He put his hands on the podium and shoved it in anger. The shove was strong enough to push the podium over, much to his surprise, and definitely to Mary's as she stood behind it.

Eric is probably two hundred pounds and five foot eight – he is bulky. Mary, on the other hand, is an elderly lady, perhaps weighing one hundred and ten pounds, standing only five foot five. The podium itself, when moved to its present position, was carried with a dolly and two people balancing and supporting it. It clears one hundred pounds empty, but when full of money, most of which coins, and numerous other items, it is not something easily moved. I tried to tip it up afterward to see how much force it required, and he was obviously a strong boy to topple it.

The podium fell over, and Mary tried to jump back, but not far enough, and the top of the podium fell on her foot. She screamed and cashiers ran to her aid, lifting the podium enough that she could pull her foot out. A manager came over and asked her if she was okay, to which she responded, "I don't think so."

This was when Eric truly snapped. He jumped on her, knocked her down and punched her face. The cashiers and manager pulled him off, and Mary went to the hospital. I saw Eric months later, and he told me he was still looking for a job, but he did not mention letting me borrow the movies again. He looked like he was doing well though, and Mary had her cast off long before then.

Some people deal with it. Some adapt. Some quit. Some just go crazy. Others write a book. Once I see how many lawsuits pend against me, I might be able to then answer who is the idiot in the relationship.

# Intellectual Intercorse

**By James**

There is probably no way to completely escape the insanity that comes with working at Wal-Mart, but there are ways to hold it off. Several staff members at our store are known for their pranks -- I happen to be one of them. Some pranks become legendary, but most are everyday jokes good for a quick laugh. The harder the day has been, the greater the odds are someone will do something to relieve the tension.

Scooter in sporting goods is perhaps the most proficient prankster in the store. One time, Assistant Manager Russ had been coming down hard on sporting goods for a couple of days, and

Scooter became sick of it. While Department Manager Brenda and he were cleaning the fishing bait, Scooter got a devilish look, and he shared his idea with Brenda.  Those two took the dead worms and loaded them in five gallon buckets, snuck them out the back door, and proceeded to pour bucket after bucket of rotting worms into the bed of Russ' pickup truck.  Scooter then pushed the worms under the tool box so Russ would not be able to see them without looking.

The funniest part is that everyone in the store was talking about it and waiting for Russ' reaction, wanting to see what would happen to Scooter once Russ found the worms.  There was just one problem: Russ did not find the worms.  Three days after the prank, Russ was in the break room, complaining that his truck smelled horribly, and Scooter literally fell off of his chair laughing. He finally told Russ what he had done, and Russ raced outside to see if it was true.  Russ made Scooter spend the next two hours cleaning out of the back of the pickup. He didn't stop laughing the whole time.

Scooter actually has had a lot of fun on Russ' behalf. One time, Scooter used industrial strength adhesive to glue a quarter to the sidewalk outside the store. He timed this so Russ would be the first to find it as he came into the store. He tried to pick it up and became agitated when he could not. He kicked at it, possibly thinking his shoe soles would snag and tear the quarter free. That failed. Ultimately, he went into the store and came back out with a hammer and chisel. He got the quarter, though it was bent and had the glue still attached with bits of concrete. He approached Scooter then, saying, "I got the quarter. I got the quarter," in a taunting tone. Russ did this all on company time.

Then there was the time Scooter signed Russ up for the Marines. Russ is a little old for such a role, though. Scooter has said to me, "I would have loved to see Russ's and the recruiter's face when the recruiter showed up at his house expecting an eighteen year old Russ. It would have been awesome."

Scooter has also pulled pranks on other assistant managers. Once, he placed a rubber spider on a spring in a filing cabinet in the manager's office. When the cabinet was opened, it sprung out.

But there was one prank too much for even Scooter to do more then play lookout. This was done to the old store manager, before Chad's time. His name was Joey, and it was his birthday. The perpetrators of this great whammy shrink-wrapped Joey's chair, desk, computer, and everything else in the office. Then, they filled the room with balloons from floor to ceiling. The door was also shrink-wrapped shut, and super glue was put into key hole. Joey was not very popular.

It took Joey an hour to get his office door open, and when it opened, the balloons flew everywhere as they were under tension. He found everything inside shrink wrapped as well. Joey was plenty torched by then, but the perpetrators were not yet through. When

Joey went to his car at the day's end, he found that it too had been shrink-wrapped. And, of course, this all was done on the clock. People got paid for this, as they should.

While I love these stories, my favorite pranks to pull are the ones that are fast, harmless, and are more or less spur of the moment. Often, they involve the PA System -- the way I figure it, if I am going to do something, I might as well let the whole store in on it. The day I came up with the "page them to their own phone" routine, I had no idea how many times my co-workers and I would be able to use it for a laugh. The idea is to pick another associate, preferably one busy enough to not think about the PA, and page them to call their own phone. The first time I did this, Cashier Desiree was targeted.

"Cashier Desiree, please dial 201. Cashier Desiree, please dial 201. Thank you." I hung up the phone and watched. Sure enough, she stopped what she was doing, picked up the phone, and dialed 201, the phone number she was calling from. Hearing the busy signal, she slammed it down, spun toward produce, and flipped me off -- right as a customer walked up to her register.

Before she quit this past September, Desiree transferred to produce. This added a new dimension to the jokes we could play on her. One day, while working in the deli, John called the store with my cell phone and asked for produce. Desiree answered, "Produce, this is Desiree, how can I help you?"

John disguised his voice, but not overly so, as he said, "Yeah, how much is one banana?"

"Are you serious?"

"Ma'am, I'm extremely serious. I'm hungry, but not too hungry."

"Well, let me find out for you. For a pound, it's forty-six cents."

"I don't need a pound. I just need the one banana."

At this point, Desiree set down the phone and walked to the bananas, where she picked three and took them to the scales. She weighed each individually and then got back on the phone. She tried to stop smiling as she said, "All right, sir. I weighed three of them, and they range from .3 to .4 pounds."

"So, that would cost me a quarter or so?"

"Probably not even."

"I'm not good at math."

"Well, I will figure it out for you, sir."

"All right. I'll try to come down in a little while."

"Well, sir, I leave in a couple minutes, but I'm sure that you can ask the two guys in the deli if you need any assistance."

At this point, John knew he had been busted, but he tried his best to follow through. "That's all right, ma'am. I can grab my own banana. Plus, my tire is flat on my bike, so who knows if I'll make it or not. You have a good night."

"You too, John."

After he hung up, he walked past her, and she started yelling at him. I used my phone to call Chris in produce, who happened to have the day off, and told him about John's call. Chris called the store then and asked her how much a case of pomegranates would cost. She checked because she could not prove it was us. After hanging up, she walked by me, flipping me the finger again and said, "Have a great night. If anyone calls wanting to know how much a pistachio is, it's not me." She seemed pretty mad. I guess that the pranks only keep some of us sane longer -- they push the others closer to their breaking points.

# Too Lazy to Read

**By James**

Wal-Mart is the only place I have ever encountered people too lazy to read for themselves. This fact is apparent throughout the store, starting with the "Entry" and "Exit" signs marking each door. I do not know how many times I have been glared at, grunted at, or straight out insulted by someone going the wrong direction when I was using them correctly. I have been able to read these two particular words since before starting school.

The reading problem is also visible in customers' inability to find items clearly marked by large signs hanging from the ceiling. For instance, the grocery signs are two and a half feet long by two and a half feet tall, and visible halfway across the store. They are marked with words such as "Bread" and "Toilet Paper." Still, customers constantly ask where the bread and other products are located. I usually point to the sign and respond, "I'm pretty sure it's in aisle one, under the big sign that says 'Bread.' That's where I would look."

But maybe the signs are just too big, because if that same bread rings up for three cents more than labeled, the customer displays the ability to read the half inch price tag in the bread aisle and remember that price for the two hours it took to finish shopping. Typically, it is the cashier's fault then.

When I worked in the meat department, customers would ask me how many grams of fat were in a package of meat. I did what normal people would do, which is flipping the package over to read the nutritional information label *on the package*. They could easily have done it themselves, but they likely thought I get paid to read for them.

In the deli, the illiteracy of the average customer is mind numbing. The hot case is where we display cooked food while keeping it warm, and it is not given such a name whimsically – the reason: it is hot. The concept is simple enough; however, to ensure some idiot does not burn themselves, there are posted signs that read, of all things, "CAUTION: HOT." That should deter people from touching it, but it often does not.

I watched a man walk to the hot case and lean against it to order. He suddenly jumped back, shaking his hands vigorously, and said, "Son of a bitch! That's hot! You guys could at least post a sign or something!" I pointed to the sign and smiled, then asked what I could get him. He walked away, shaking his head at me, like I was the idiot in the relationship.

And it is not just the "CAUTION: HOT" sign people refuse to read, as boards that post every item we serve and how much each item costs, are typically overlooked. Without fail, someone asks every day what each item is in the case, and then inevitably asks how much each costs. I like to point at the sign and say, "Let's see, the boneless barbeque wings are $4.48 a pound. And the sign here also says that the popcorn chicken is $3.97 a pound." When someone sees me read the sign and still asks about another item, I begin to read the entire board. Some people become annoyed by this, but it is easier and saves me time.

This seems to happen everywhere in the store. I cannot even guess how many times a customer has brought me an item to ask its cost. One gentleman waited patiently through three customers to ask a price of something outside my department. I had no idea how much it cost, so I left the deli and had him show me where he found it. He pointed to the shelf tag and said, "Right there." I read out loud the price on the shelf tag for his answer. I felt bad for the guy, but after this happened several times with different people, I grew immune to the embarrassment of their stupidity. There are some who even watch me read a price, and then they point to the next label and ask for that item's price.

In the deli, the eight piece chicken baskets and rotisserie chickens are clearly marked with the time they finish cooking so customers know how fresh they are; still, most customers ask when they were made. I respond, "Oh, didn't we mark the time on that one? Oh, yeah, we did." I point to the time and make the person read it themselves, though sometimes the customer will then ask if the time is correct. "I would assume so," I respond.

While it often seems no one in Wal-Mart can read, some customers are the exact opposite and want to read everything. These people will come to the deli and ask to see a package of unopened meat to read the ingredients. They will analyze the grams of fat and nutrients in each serving before finally asking for their meat. This practice can be frustrating if I am busy, but I have no real gripe with these people. I only want to demonstrate there are always exceptions to the rule. Sometimes, I do need these reminders.

Customers have even asked to see the food holding log, where we write the exact time anything is cooked and at what temperature it finishes. My first week in the deli, I had no idea customers were not allowed see the log as it is protected under the Wal-Mart confidentiality clause. I let a man look at the boneless barbeque wings' time and temp. It had been a little over an hour since they were cooked, but he saw the temperature was 202 degrees. He said, "Jesus. That's too hot. I'll get the popcorn chicken." The popcorn chicken had been in there longer but had only temped around 170. Never mind that, once in the case, the food will be around the same temperature.

# Customer Responsibility

**By R.A. Wilson**

I hate walking into this place, but it is safer than being outside. I always question peoples' ability to drive, but a quick jaunt through the parking lot removes all doubt of their ability – they have none. I cannot even begin to guess how many times a car has almost hit me in front of the store.

When I drove in today, I followed a car for a few blocks. Other than speeding up and slamming on the brakes the last second to avoid running a red light, the driver did not seem too dangerous – until I watched her cut off someone to turn into the store's parking lot. The oncoming traffic slammed on their brakes, leaving rubber on the road, barely missing a collision. Feeling shaken, I waited for traffic to pass before turning into the parking lot.

I could tell the store was busy by the sheer number of people entering and exiting the building. The car I followed sped toward the masses, not even slowing as it approached the crosswalk. I became rigid upon realizing it was not going to stop. The car's brake lights came on for less than a second before zigzagging through the families and slow moving old folk in the crosswalk.

It was the scariest thing I have ever seen here. Customers do not typically look for oncoming traffic, almost like they believe cars will stop, but most drivers do not look for pedestrians either. I have seen on occasion where drivers slam on their brakes to not hit someone, scaring the crap out of everyone involved. But not this driver. She saw the people; she just preferred to drive around them like cones on a track. Maybe it was for the challenge, because I bet moving cones would be more difficult to not hit.

This store has not just one but *two* crosswalks, and she did this twice. Finally parking, I noticed the other car near me, and I glared at it in disbelief more than anger. The driver stepped out. It was Kelly from the photo lab. She was in such a hurry to reach work she almost killed thirty people. That is commitment, so much that she should be committed to a mental hospital.

It almost prompted laughter when she did not bother

looking for traffic at the crosswalk. Apparently, she expected nobody to drive like her; either that or she has such faith in others that it did not scare her. Knowing her, though, Kelly's narcissism probably left her thinking nobody matters other than her, so they should not be concerned with.

I stopped at the crosswalk and saw two trucks coming. One passed by, but the others was far enough that I started forward. Five steps later, the truck nearly ran over my leg and took my ass off as he zipped behind me. I twirled around and saw it was a high school kid driving a rusted Blazer. Subwoofers were booming, and the truck was going at least twenty-five and did not bother to even slow for me. I realize that, unlike Kelly, he did not bother to swerve either. The insanity baffled me, but I am glad to still be standing.

As I said, I hate walking into this place, but it is a lot safer then the parking lot. I head to the time clock and start my day. I am surprised as I am actually early.

*12:56.* Nine hours and four minutes, minus my one hour lunch.

I walk onto the floor of electronics and over to the counter, where I find Becky standing with a customer. The gentleman is leaning against the battery kiosk, a large cube with a giant plastic AA battery on the top. Its four sides are teeming with batteries, and frankly, it is such an eyesore that it is hard to miss.

The customer sounds annoyed as he asks Becky, "Where are

90

the batteries?"

When asked such an obviously stupid question, one's mind plays a trick. The first reaction is to think he must be joking. This accounts for the first second of silence. The second reaction is the realization he is serious. Again, another second. One immediately thinks of a sarcastic answer, but the next two seconds are filled with arguing as to why giving said answer is a bad idea.

Becky ultimately decides to not verbalize her response at all. After five seconds of uncomfortable silence, she merely points to the kiosk he leans against. As they say, silence can say more than words, making her response perhaps the best option, mocking yet not incriminating.

He looks down to the kiosk and smiles. "I should feel ashamed," he says.

Becky and I look at each other and quickly walk away. At the electronics register, she says to me, "Mostly they just haven't been able to find CDs today. That's one for the record books."

I smile. "Have a lot of people looking for Kelly Clarkson been searching in the R's?" I have learned that knowing one's alphabet is not a requirement to shop here.

"Not Kelly, Hinder. The customer asked me where Hinder was. I told him in the H's, but that wasn't good enough. He said he couldn't find it. So I walked over there, thinking that perhaps we were out. But no, it was right where it should have been. And there was not just one. We have about ten sitting in plain sight."

I stifle a laugh. "The longer I work here, the less faith I have in humans as a species. One and a half billion years of evolution, and this is the outcome. It's quite sad, really. It's almost enough to make me question Darwin." I wink at her. "Almost enough." I share with her my story about Kelly's driving, and we both have a good laugh. Stupidity is humorous after the fact, though frustrating and sometimes scary during.

I start working directs, which is freight shipped from manufacturers and not warehouse – *directly*. I work through a box of DVD's, sorting them into piles matching the different shelves. I take new releases first, and as I put them out, a customer approaches.

"Do you have *Over the Hedge*?"

I look at her, confused. "The game or movie?"

"The movie. I saw the poster by the front doors."

"That poster is for the video game, which was released a week ago, but the movie is coming to theaters this Friday."

"I saw an ad for it yesterday that said it was coming out."

"To theaters."

"No, I think it was to video."

"I'm sorry, but no. It won't be out on video for at least eight months."

"Then why is the game out?"

"Games typically come out before the movie even goes to theaters."

"So I can't get it?" she asks again.

"Only the video game. We don't have the movie."

I was bewildered when first asked for a movie just coming to theaters, thinking it an odd occurrence, but it happens every time a big name movie is released. Most people ignore what is said after ads, which tells both the date of release and to what medium, be it DVD or theaters. I expect to be asked for *Over the Hedge* twice more today, as I was yesterday, and will be tomorrow. In fact, this will carry on for about two weeks until finally tapering off. It will happen again toward the end of the movie's run in theaters, still some months before the DVD release.

I continue putting away directs, working through a couple boxes. During this time, Becky leaves for lunch, and I am interrupted on nine occasions. Four of these require a walk to the front with videogames, two are for questions about digital audio players, one is for portable DVD players, and the last is about Tracfones. Of course, there are random questions about item location, to which I usually just point to the big signs hanging from the ceiling marking the locales. These take little time to shoo the customer away. I know I should take them to the item myself, but I'm not actually allowed to leave electronics unless taking something up front.

When I start the next box, another customer approaches me. "Do you have under the counter radios?" he asks.

"You would think we would as I get asked that twice a week, but we don't. My department manager tells me we can't even order them."

"So you don't have them?"

"No, we don't."

"None with a CD player."

"We don't have any."

"Not even just a radio?"

"Nope."

"Oh, because I want one for my wife. When she cooks, she turns up the radio in the living room, and it disturbs everyone. I figure if I get an under the counter radio, it would make her happy, and the rest of the house won't be so annoyed."

"I'd try Karl's, or maybe RadioShack. Either of them might carry under the counter radios."

"So you don't have any then, not even with a cassette player?"

"We don't have any kind. Radios, CD's, or anything else."

"Okay then. Thanks for your help."

He walks away, but I know he wants to ask again. Why is it when I tell someone we do not have something, they ask again, just in a different way, and then do it again? It is always followed by the

94

story of why they want it, and right after they ask again. Are they expecting me to be the idiot, like I do not understand their question? Or maybe am I to break from my *lying* under the scrutiny of multiple questions? I saw that on some cop show once. I think it was *Reno 911*.

*3:07*. I decide to take a break, needing to escape the floor. Allison watches the department while I am gone.

*3:31*. After my fifteen minute break, I return to the floor. Allison had left after Becky came back from lunch.

A customer grabs my attention as soon as I step into the department. He is a young boy, perhaps about eleven, who desperately "needs" a video game. I follow him to the game case, and he points to *Grand Theft Auto: San Andreas*. Annoyance fills me, but I believe I hide it well.

I say to him, "I'll take this up front for you. When you check out, just tell your cashier this is waiting for you."

"I want to pay back here," he says.

I hold in a sigh as I look down at him. "Because the game is rated M for mature, I *need* your parent to tell me if it is okay to sell this to you."

"I'll go get my mom." He runs off.

I take the game to the register and wait. A minute later, the phone rings. "This is electronics. How can I help you?"

An old man's voice greets me from the other end. "Yes,

someone told me you have a radio with two cassette players for twenty dollars." It sounds like his mouth is too far from the receiver, making me strain to hear his question.

"Are you talking about a boom box?" At that price, I cannot imagine it would be otherwise, but I do not remember any with a dual cassette player.

"I don't know. Someone just told me you had a stereo with two cassette players for twenty dollars." Though I barely hear him, I can discern aggravation in his voice.

"I'll look to see what we have for you. I'm going to put you on hold for a minute." I push hold and place the receiver down and leave the register. The stereos are all on the same wall, and I start looking where the boom boxes are located. Not one has dual cassettes, as I guessed, so I move onto the shelf systems. I find a few here, but the cheapest runs at $149. Whoever he talked with was mistaken.

I walk back to the register and pick up the phone, but the line has been disconnected. I assume he got tired of waiting even though it was not even two minutes. I hang the phone back up and see the young boy coming with his mom.

"He said you wouldn't sell him a game," she accuses.

I blink and stare at her for two seconds before responding. "It's rated mature, so I can't sell it to someone younger then seventeen without parental consent."

96

"That's a stupid rule. It's just a videogame."

"It's corporate policy based on the accepted ESRB rating scale."

"A game is not like cigarettes. It can't hurt him."

I imagine she means that videogames are not a controlled drug, which is true, but the point she wants to make is still wrong. Videogames are much the same as controlled drugs when it comes to selling them, and our policies are clearly posted for sales of either. Tobacco is federally controlled, removing the ability to bend the rules, but to be fair, games are a different matter. Corporate decided to follow the ESRB guidelines, which means we can be somewhat flexible.

When I say flexible, this means if you look old enough, I might forgo checking your ID for a videogame. With tobacco and alcohol, if you do not look twenty-seven, I am going to check, and I might even want to see ID's of those with you if buying alcohol. The fact of the matter is, I will not sell a mature rated game to someone that obviously is not even a teenager regardless of how much they complain.

It is the customer's responsibility to prove they are old enough to buy age restricted items. I know. It is a crazy idea, the notion that a customer should be responsible for something in this deal. It is also the mother's responsibility to make sure her child is not playing games outside his maturity. Many people complain about the graphic nature of games, but the truth of the matter is the rating scale works well; it is in the parents' end that it fails.

"You don't mind if he buys this game then?"

"Of course not."

I sell the game, and she huffs off with her child following close behind, smiling as he holds onto his game like it might run away. He is probably thinking about running over people, shooting others, and buying hookers. The dreams of an eight year old.

My phone rings again. I answer it, only half thinking of what I am saying until the voice on the other end speaks. It is the old man looking for the dual cassette player.

"Why did you hang up on me?" he asks.

I already know I am not going to enjoy this phone call. "I didn't hang up on you. I put you on hold."

"You hung up on me, now don't do it again. Do you have a radio with two cassette players? Someone told me you do for twenty dollars."

Here we go again. "No, we do not. The cheapest one we have runs for one-hundred fifty dollars."

"You're wrong. Someone told me that you have one for twenty dollars."

I am obviously not getting through to this old man. "Would you like me to look again for you?" I ask, knowing we do not have what he wants.

"Do that, but don't hang up on me."

"I didn't hang up one you. Now, if you will just wait one minute, I'll be back with you." I set the receiver down on the counter, not putting him on hold this time. Maybe his phone plays music instead of a dial tone when the line is dead. I can see how that might create some confusion.

I walk back to the stereo wall, knowing it a waste of energy. I look again, and I am surprised. It has not changed since five minutes ago. Back at the counter, I pick up the receiver.

"We don't have one at that price. The cheapest runs for one-hundred fifty dollars."

"Are you sure, because someone told me you have a stereo with two cassette players for twenty bucks?"

"I'm sure we don't have a dual cassette player at that price. Perhaps they saw it on WalMart.com. They carry more there then we can in our store."

"Fine. Now I'm going to hang up on you." *Click.*

I am now pissed off, but I gently hang up the phone and walk away from the register. I check my watch.

*5:37.* Gleefully, I head to lunch. I spend this time typing to make sure I remember this day.

*6:53.* Three hours and seven minutes. Becky goes home, leaving me alone once more.

The service desk pages me to the front, and as I am on my

way, a shopper exits an aisle while not looking. She would have happily rammed her cart into my side and probably glared at me for it had I not leapt out of the way. She still glares at me as if I am acting like an idiot. She says nothing though and keeps on her way.

I see a TV box sitting on a shopping cart as I reach the service desk. "What's up?" I ask Sara, the associate helping the woman with her TV.

"She wants to bring the TV back."

"Does she have a receipt?"

The customer answers, "No."

I turn to the lady now. "When did you buy the TV?"

"I didn't buy it. It was a present."

"When was it bought?"

"About five months ago, but I just tried it yesterday and there is a green bar through the picture."

"Five months ago?"

"Yes, but I just tried it yesterday."

I want to reject this return. Our policy is 90 days for most returns, and I have no need to count the days out on my fingers to know she is a little late. I can sympathize though, because she could be telling the truth about not using it yet, however unlikely. On the other hand, I am not sure how someone could let a TV sit around for five months and never use it once, but I will give her the benefit of doubt as she seems nice. I would consider the return if she has the receipt as we no longer carry the TV, keeping me from knowing its cost.

"Can you get the receipt from whoever bought it for you?"

"They probably don't have it anymore, and they live out of state."

"Have you asked if they have it? They could mail it to you."

"I can't call them. My cell phone doesn't have long distance."

I am starting to not like this lady now, and not because she is becoming difficult, but because all she is offering are excuses that make no sense. I for one have never heard of a cell phone that does not have long distance. Naturally, I think she is lying to me about something.

"I can't do anything without the receipt, and even if you had it, I still might not be able to return the TV."

"Why not?" she interrupts to ask what I was about to explain.

"We don't carry this TV anymore, so I don't have a replacement for it, nor do I know how much it's worth. And we only offer returns up to 90 days."

"I think it was two hundred. You could just give me that and we call it even."

Now I am not willing to work with her at all. She has no proof it was bought here, and I have no idea how much it really is worth. "I'm sorry, but without a receipt, I can't do anything for you. I would recommend contacting the manufacturer to see what they can do, but without the receipt, they won't honor the warranty."

"So what am I supposed to do? Am I stuck with a broken TV?"

"You're only stuck with a broken TV if you hold onto it and do nothing. Contact the manufacturer, and they might be able to help you."

She was mad now, and I was not willing to waste more time trying to make her happy, mostly because I cannot make her happy. I tell her to have a good day and good luck before heading back to electronics. She is angry with me since I did not fix her problem, but she should be mad with herself. I did what I was supposed to do; she failed at her responsibility.

And here we are again. Customers have responsibility in all that is done here. Our return policy is easy to understand. 90 days is the maximum for any return, and receipts are not even always needed. The customer is responsible to prove the item was bought from Wal-Mart, hence the receipt is the easiest way as one needs to just keep it. Furthermore, they must bring back not only the item itself but everything that came with it. In the case of TV's, the manual and remote control need to come back as well.

Associates are blamed when returns are rejected, but they are only rejected when the customer does not take care of their responsibilities.

I leave the lady complaining to Sara. I feel bad for this, but she knows how to handle such people. Sara has faced harder challenges. Fun fact, she was almost a professional soccer player. Maybe Sara will kick her. That would make me feel better.

I check my watch.

*8:06*. One hour and fifty-four minutes left.

I walk to the TV wall as I see three people looking up at them. The short gentleman of the trio points to our sixty-one inch Panasonic LCD projection TV. "I want that," he says.

This will be the first one I sell since we received them a few months ago, and I have wanted to sell one, mostly as a thing of pride. I page receiving and tell them I need the TV brought out, but they do not seem as impressed as I am.

As usual, it takes about twenty minutes for the TV to be brought onto the floor. I tender the transaction at my register, and using a pallet jack, I walk to TV to the front of the store. On my way by, I tell a CSM to call a courtesy associate, preferably Darold, to help load it for the customer.

Darold meets me at the door, and we follow the three to their vehicle. We approach a brand new Ford F-250. It's Ford Red and beautiful. We reach the truck, but the customer keeps walking around it to a rusted Ford Aerostar on the other side of the truck. The van has broken windows with vinyl taped over them. The

103

customer opens the back hatch after yanking on the latch a couple times and looks at us expectantly as he holds the door up. Evidently, the gas struts are no good.

Darold and I gaze into the rear. There is so much garbage that I doubt the TV will fit, but the other two jump inside and start kicking the crap out of the way. Darold and I lift the TV and slide it into the van's rear, plowing through the cans, cups, dirty rags, and other things that I do not want to identify. The shorter man closes the hatch, slamming it three times before it catches.

He thanks us for the help before Darold and I begin to walk to the store. Behind us, I hear the van's starter turning the engine over, and over, and over. It becomes silent, and then he tries to start it again. No luck. The van will not start. Darold nearly falls over laughing, but I keep walking. I want nothing else to do with those three clowns.

How screwed up can someone's priorities be? Who buys a twenty-six hundred dollar television when their car does not even start? I return to the store and head back to electronics. Darold takes the pallet jack to put it away for me.

*9:07.* Fifty-three minutes left.

I start to walk the department for my final zoning, making sure the floor is clear and merchandise is put away correctly. The department looks good after about twenty minutes of work, so I decide to organize the dump bin. This is where the assortment of

$5.50 DVD's are kept. We actually organize it almost every day, and sometimes twice a day, though it never actually looks like we do, but that is because customers tend to be horrible slobs. I can spend nearly an hour cleaning the bin, and two minutes after I am done, I have seen customers grabbing handfuls of DVD's and throwing them.

At this time of night, a quick fix can keep it looking good until about noon the next day. I dive into it... well, not really dive in it, because that would be stupid. Other then the obvious reasons why this would be stupid, most people do not have an inkling of what can be found in there.

Typically, I find DVDs that don't belong, like new releases that prompt calls from cashiers with customers demanding twenty dollar DVDs for $5.50. We do not cave in to that. Other items are found commonly, like shoes, pens, dolls, tools, infant toys, CD's, popsicles, pizzas, makeup, wigs, empty Icee cups, packaging from stolen items, quarts of oil, fishing bait, travel pillows, squishy rubber balls from toys. Sometimes, even more grotesque things are found, like condoms (never a used one yet), but the worst had to be the dirty diapers. I do not know how they ended up in there, how someone decided that was a good place for them. I actually have nothing to say for this. I just don't know. Dirty diapers?

Suddenly, Assistant Manager Alex runs by with a comforter from the shelf, pulling it out of the packaging, and he looks upset.

Curious, I step into the back room and see him enter the management office, and then two police officers enter behind him with other members of management.

I casually walk by the management office, trying to see inside, but the door is closed and the glass is covered. I see Caleb in receiving, and he is talking with a couple others. He too looks upset.

I walk up to him and ask, "What's going on?"

"Al just got the fuckin' crap beaten out of him."

I am instantly shocked. This is horrible. Al is a nice guy. If it happened to Caleb, I would assume he just pissed off the wrong person. Frankly, it is bound to happen, but not to Al. Everybody likes Al. He is such a great guy, he even sticks up for Caleb.

I found out the full story later. Al was behind the store, and a white Nissan pickup was speeding through, doing cookies. Al yelled at them to slow down, and the truck stopped. The driver got out, reeking of alcohol, and attacked. Al pushed him away twice, finding the man unbalanced, and this drunken brigand could not even knock Al's glasses off. The man got back into his truck then, and Al started to write down the license plate number, but then the driver veered toward Al. It hit him, and he went over the hood and flew five feet to land on the blacktop. The whole attack was caught on tape, and the driver was arrested a few days later.

After the attack, Al sat in the management office for almost an hour before being taken to the hospital. He had a fractured

106

ankle, wrist, elbow, skull, right stapies, and his brain was swelling. He was okay in the end, other than loosing perfect hearing in one ear and his sense of smell, but why did he have to sit in the back office with such severe injuries? The ambulance was finally called when he began to go into shock.

My fiancée, Alysia, cut the tip off one of her fingers in the deli months before, and she sat in the back for over forty-five minutes before being taken to the emergency room. I wonder how many people have died in management offices from injuries they could have survived. Oddly enough, I could not find any statistics on this.

After talking with Caleb, I turn in my keys and clock out, suffering from slight shock myself. I remember I have to do some shopping before heading home, which is okay as I do not feel like leaving the building or driving at this point. I stop in the bathroom first, and as I am washing my hands, two of the overnight maintenance guys enter the bathroom together. The guy in the lead has greasy slicked-back hair. I am not a fan of his. He walks by me to check his hair in the mirror, and then he walks out, with the other following him.

I stare at the closed door then. What just happened? The greasy haired guy walks in, with the other following, to check his hair. Did the other come in to help him, to say the back looks good? I get a little laugh at this idea, though I am a little freaked out, but maybe that is because I am still shaken about Al.

I leave the bathroom and head to the grocery end of the store. Refusing to get a cart, I walk the aisles while my arms get overfilled. I head to the front, nearly an hour after I was scheduled to leave, and I see the greasy haired maintenance guy zipping down the aisle on the floor scrubber. It is termed a floor scrubber, but most of us call it a Zambonie, because that is what it looks like.

He is speeding towards me, but I am not worried, because surely he will slow to not run over a customer. I hear him coming from behind, and I glance over my shoulder just in time to realize he is not slowing. I jump to the side as he zooms past, making me drop half of what I am carrying.

I start to pick it all up when I hear a crash ahead. Looking up, I see he ran the Zambonie into a rack of clothes and pulled it partially in the aisle behind him. He looks at it, considering what to do, but keeps driving ahead, speeding on, leaving it. I guess nowhere is safe.

# Associopaths III

**By James**

It is my final break of the night. I enter the break room, thinking it is going to be a waste of fifteen minutes of my life, until I see Scooter. He has a gravity about him, but that could be the fact he is shaped like a small planet. He always has the best stories though – and he is always willing to tell them to anyone who will listen. Normally, I make him tell me the story of how his brother pushed him out of the tree house, causing him to fall twelve feet onto a pile of boards with rusty nails. Today, I ask a question I have wanted to ask for days. "Hey, Scott, what's the worst injury you've ever gotten at Wal-Mart?"

"Without a doubt, the time that I was stabbed in the head with a peg hook."

"What?" I am already laughing.

"Yeah. This one time I was working with Nora, and she had apparently taken wire cutters to one of the peg hooks so it would be shorter. She was using it to hang up the Garvey Gun used for pricing merchandise under the sporting goods counter. Well, I didn't realize this, and as I was making change for this old lady, who was asking me a ton of unnecessary questions, I dropped a dollar on the floor. I leaned down to pick it up, and I stabbed myself in the head with that goddamn peg hook, right here." He points to a spot about an inch above his right eye.

"Blood is showering everywhere. It's all over my face, and it gets on the counter. I cover it with my hand, and it's streaming through my fingers. I'm in a lot of pain, and Nora tells me to head to the back and get it looked at. As I start to leave, this damn old lady grabs my arm and says, 'Where are you going? You haven't answered my question!' I'm bleeding all over, even on this lady and her money, yet she demands that I answer her question. I couldn't believe it. Norma ran interference for me to get her off my back."

He slams his hand on the table in frustration. "And then when I got to the management office, they wouldn't let me go to the hospital to get it looked at until I finished all of the damn paper work first. I was back there, bleeding, for a good thirty minutes. I ended up getting three stitches, but I had to take a drug test at the clinic before they did anything! They said it could be either urine or blood, so of course I said blood, but then they grabbed a needle. What the hell, there's blood everywhere! Why did they need a needle?"

"Why did you have to take a drug test for stitches?"

"Oh, Wal-Mart policy. That way, if I'm on drugs of any sort, they don't have to cover me."

"That's crazy."

"No, it's a good policy, I suppose."

"I meant your story."

"Oh. Yeah, that was the worst one. I've had a lot of injuries, though. I think I still hold the record for most injuries while working at Wal-Mart – or at least at this store. Did I ever tell you about the time I got electrocuted? Russ thought that was pretty funny."

"Electrocuted?"

"Yeah, I was in electronics helping Patty put together a new camera bar. I'm hooking up the main console and I said, 'All right, I'm hooking it up. Wait till I say now.' And all I hear is 'Okay, now!' They tell me that every light in electronics flickered. I don't know. I just remember waking up with Assistant Manager Russ standing over me, grinning, while I'm laying on the floor in the fetal position. Patty was bawling hysterically in the back."

"Did management make you sit in the back again?"

"Kind of...but it was more like they just let me lay down on the counter in the management office for a half hour."

I see my break is over, and as I stand to leave, Scooter says, "Oh, hey, you know I have that heart condition, right? The day after Christmas last year, I started having chest pains. I go to the training room to tell Fran, who offers to drive me to the hospital so I don't have to pay for an ambulance. As we're walking out, Assistant Manager Sylvia says, 'Scott, I just had an associate call in sick. When you get back from the emergency room, can you work a double shift?'"

"I give her a look that says, 'You crazy bitch,' but I don't say anything."

# Deli Style

**By James**

I slowly chant to myself as I enter the store, "My next job will *not* be customer service. My next job will *not* be customer service." I suddenly realize I literally have no idea which day of the week it is. Today is not Sunday, because that carries the pseudo-joy of making more than ten dollars an hour to be here. I realize further it really does not matter -- every day here is the same.

I make my way slowly to the back, mostly because I cannot get around the people spontaneously stopping through the aisles. I pass an elderly lady talking to herself, and two children appear out of nowhere to slam into my leg. I apologize for being in their way, and they continue running, never looking back at me. I did not mean to apologize, but I am used to doing so when on the clock, making my response out of habit more than courtesy. I do not know how many times I have smiled and said hello to customers when off the clock. They just see a fellow customer smiling incessantly at them and asking how they are doing. They probably think I am some random idiot... and they might be right.

I make my way through Electronics and toward layaway and see a couple people standing at layaway who probably will not be helped anytime soon. They look at me like puppies in a pound, begging for me to save them. I avert my eyes and continue through the door to the back. I swipe my badge on the time clock at 1:45 and walk into the break room to sit next to Chris. I say, "What's up, man?"

"You guys are getting pounded up there." Great. Another wonderful day in the deli. I sit in the back until Chris's fifteen minute break is over. It is 2:04 as we leave and start toward the front of the store. We walk through the back for as long as possible to avoid customers.

As we pass the door where I came in, I see those customers still standing at layaway. With no one helping them. If I was not running late, I would page someone to help them.

When I arrive at the deli, a woman stands at the meat case, waiting for help while three of my co-workers are out of sight by the sink in the back, jibber jabbing and "sampling." None of them seem to be able to help this customer. She asks me, "Can I get some meat?"

I wash my hands and put on gloves before walking to the case. "What can I do for you?"

She says, "Well, I need a pound of turkey and a pound of ham. I'll be back."

As she starts to leave, I say, "Which kind of turkey would you like?"

She looks at me like I am crazy. "How many do you have?"

I show her the selection of turkey, including oven roasted, sun dried tomato, hickory smoked, honey smoked, regular smoked, peppered, cracked pepper, honey, and turkey pastrami. Most of these come in various forms due to separate brand names and distributors. All in all, there are fifteen different types of turkey. She says, "I'll take... this one," pointing to the one she wants.

Unfortunately, I cannot see which one she points at. Either it is hickory, honey, or smoked. I say, "Sorry, but I really can't see which one you're pointing at."

She sighs and says, "I want the smoked one." I grab the regular smoked turkey and she says, "No! The *hickory* smoked one."

I smile and apologize, then ask, "How would you like this sliced?"

"Yes, please."

"How thick would you like it sliced?"

"No. I want it thin."

I cut a slice and show it to her. "No. Thinner." I cut it thinner and I hear, "No. Thinner." I shave a slice and she says, "I guess that will do." I cut the pound and bag it. Then she says, "And then the ham."

I say, "And which ham would you like?"

"Well, how many hams could you possibly have?" I point to the eight kinds of ham, and she says, "I'll take that one."

Again, I have to remind her I cannot see what she is pointing at.

"The honey ham." She wants it cut the same way as the turkey. I bag it, price it, and send her on her way.

I notice a lady standing at the hot case, waving her hand at flies without really noticing them. I walk over to help her as my co-workers are still "too busy" and out of sight. She says, "Do you have okra?"

"No. We didn't get any on the truck today."

"Why not? Didn't you order it?"

"Yes, my manager did order…."

"Oh, so you don't know then."

"Excuse me?"

"Well, you didn't order it, so how would you know if he did?"

"I watched her while she was placing the order."

"You went out of your way to watch whether she ordered the okra or not?"

"No, ma'am. I just meant I saw her when she was ordering. Is there anything else I can get for you?"

"Yeah. Give me some of the barbeque tenders."

"Did you say you wanted the boneless barbeque wings or the chicken tenders?"

"The wings." I put some in the container and she leaves. I turn back and another customer approaches the hot case. He grabs an eight piece chicken and says, "Can I pay for this up here?"

"No, we don't have a register back here. You'll have to take it to the cash registers over there."

"Which one?"

"Any of them." I think better of this statement and say, "Any of the ones where you see a cashier."

"So not the self-checkouts?"

"Oh, yeah, you can take it there too." He grabs the chicken and scampers off to the cash registers as I hear the bell ding at the meat counter. I find an elderly woman there. I say, "What can I do for you, ma'am?"

She looks directly at me but says nothing at all. I wait patiently, and she continues to ignore me. This is always an awkward feeling.

I start to turn away, intending to get some cleaning done while I wait for her to make up her mind, when she says, "Can I get some help?"

I turn back to her. "Sure, what can I do for you?"

"I need meat."

"Well then, you've come to the right place. What kind are you looking for?"

"Beef."

I reach from one end of the roast beef section to the other as I say, "Well, our roast beef runs from here to here. We have several different kinds. Is there a particular one you were looking for?"

"Crap. That's a lot." She pauses for twenty seconds while looking each over. "What's the difference between them?"

I never know what to say exactly to this question; it is not like I went to meat school or something. "Well, the regular roast beef is pretty much just regular roast beef. The top round is a higher quality cut of roast beef...."

She points to the first one, "So this one is shitty then?"

"Well, I wouldn't say that, it's just not as high quality...."

"So it's shitty. What's the Cajun roast beef like?"

"It's a little spicier, but not really hot."

"Hmm.... What about this Angus one?"

"That's the highest quality roast beef we carry. It's a lot

like…."

"It's expensive."

"Yes, it is a bit more expensive."

She leans in like if she is to scold a small child. "A bit? It's a buck higher. Is it worth it?"

"I think it is."

She scowls at me, completely convinced I only say that because I want her to spend more money. Maybe she believes I work on a meat commission.

"I'll take this first one."

*The shitty one?* I think to myself. "And how would you like that cut?"

"Sliced."

"Good call. Would you like it thin, thick, in between the two, or shredded?"

"It's for sandwiches."

Before I worked here, I had no clue people thought there was a set thickness for sandwich meat. I randomly guess at what this particular customer thinks the "sandwich" setting is, and I show her a slice.

"Like this here, or thicker or thinner than that?"

"I said 'sandwich,' didn't I?"

"You did indeed, ma'am, but customers seem to have varying opinions on what exactly 'sandwich' is."

"Then that will do."

"All right. And how much did you want today?"

"Let's go a half pound."

I slice five pieces when she stops me and says, "Well, maybe a little thinner than that."

I cut it a little thinner and say, "More like this?"

"Thinner."

I cut another. "Like this?"

"Thinner."

I cut another.

"That will do," she finally says.

"Awesome." I bag the meat and it comes to .52 pounds, and I print the tag.

"You went over, huh?"

"Yeah, it's hard to be exact all the time."

"Maybe you'll try harder next time."

"Here's your meat. Will you need anything else today?"

"No, I think I've wasted enough time over here."

"Alright. Well, have a good night." She ignores me as she walks away. I really hate my job.

# A Sporting Chance: The Ballard of Scooter

### By R.A. Wilson

When I first met Scooter, I thought he was loud, obnoxious, and an idiot. After knowing him, I realize he is just loud, obnoxious, and an idiot with funny stories. He will be the first person to admit he is loud and obnoxious. As for an idiot, I do not mean he is stupid. Far from it; he has just done some really idiotic things.

As good as the stories about Scooter are, he has told me some about other associates and customers that had me falling out of my chair in laughter. He was department manager of electronics before Allison, and Joeltron started in electronics under Scooter. Joeltron (then just Joel) was cleaning the TV screens with window cleaner and paper towels, using an aluminum ladder to reach the shelves. Scooter recommended shutting off the TVs before cleaning them. Joel did not.

The reason Scooter recommended shutting off the TV is a simple one. The "tube" television is actually called a CRT, or cathode ray tube. A cathode ray is a beam of positively charged particles used to create TV images, but this attracts a large negative charge on the outside of the screen. When Joeltron wiped the screens, the negative charge passed to him as static electricity. And when his hand touched the metal ladder, there was an arching snap of light. It shocked Joeltron so badly that he almost fell off the ladder.

Nora, who worked in the department then, did the same thing, but she did fall from the ladder and onto the concrete floor. Sitting in the personal office afterward, Scooter said to her, "I give you a seven."

"A seven?" Nora asked.

"It was ten on the dive, but you didn't get your legs together on the reentry."

Nora laughed, but Cleo from personnel hit him with a clip board.

Back in those days, the videogame case was different. The company had just changed from a locking metal rack to the glass cases. These older glass doors slid shut and locked, overlapping a few inches. Once, Scooter found a young boy had slid his hand between the overlapping doors and grabbed a videogame inside the case. Once in hand, he could not pull his arm back out. He was struggling with this when Scooter approached him.

The boy demanded, "Open the door."

Scooter shook his head and laughed. "Let go of the game."

"Open the case."

"No. Drop the game."

The boy then tried to remove the game with only two fingers holding it, but that still was too wide to fit through the small opening. "Open the case."

"Drop the game," Scooter reasserted. "I can't open it with your arm in the doors. They slide over each other, making your hole there much smaller."

The boy's mother then came, seeing Scooter and her son arguing. "Open the case for him," she demanded.

Scooter stepped out of the way. "Look at what your son is doing."

Her face became red as she was embarrassed for her son's theft attempt. He eventually dropped the game, and his mom did not buy a game for him. Now, the glass cases latch together instead of overlap, so no one can do that anymore. Apparently, that was not an isolated incident.

Scooter obviously is no longer the manager of electronics.

That change has to do with ten thousand dollars of loss. The problem was nobody knew what was missing. Scooter, being the department manager, was the fall guy. He was blamed and demoted. It was later discovered that an employee of our distributor of CDs and some DVDs was stealing them to sell back to the store. It was too late for Scooter then, as Allison was hired in his place.

Lovable Scooter was later removed from the department all together after an argument with Allison that involved his tongue being stuck out when he blew her a raspberry. Scooter in electronics became Scooter in sporting goods. He is still the same ol' Scooter though.

Recently, three high school boys wearing letterman jackets walked through Sporting Goods and picked up a can of buck scent, which is concentrated doe urine in aerosol form used for hunting. The can acts like a grenade when the top is opened. It first fizzes, but then pops, creating a cloud of urine, and it cannot be stopped from popping once opened. Scooter watched one of the kids open the can, and the group started giggling like a group of adolescent girls talking about boys. They walked to the aisle of hunting clothes and placed the can down and walked away.

Scooter followed them, knowing they were up to something, and his rage peaked when the can was opened. He picked if off the floor and hurried after the boys, who were walking away. Scooter grabbed the one who opened the can and twirled him around. Holding the boy by the shirt, Scooter shoved the can under the kid's nose.

"You think this is funny? You think this is funny?" Scooter said.

The kid's eyes were watering as he tried to pull away, saying, "Dude."

"No." Scooter gripped tighter. "You think this is funny? Here's how it's going to work. You're gonna leave. I do not want to see you in my department again with your buddies. If I do, I'm going to call management, they're going to call the cops, and you are going to go to jail for vandalism."

"Let me go." The boy struggled a little.

"Get out." Scooter pointed in the direction of the doors, removing the buck scent from under his nose.

"You can't make me leave."

"Oh yes I can." Scooter walked him and his friends to the front and through the doors. The kid looked like he had been tear-gassed with tears streaming down his face. Scooter went to the bathroom afterward and washed his hands as the urine got all over him. The smell was nauseous, and it stuck to his hand, looking like a brown sugar gel. That rancid smell stuck in his nose, making him vomit.

The can of buck scent was the third to be opened in two

weeks time, prompting them to be placed behind the sporting goods counter.  Scooter did not know what was happening the first time he saw one go off in the department as he had never actually seen one used before. It was sitting in the middle of sporting goods, hissing. Scooter went to pick the buck scent up to put it away, and when he was standing over the can, it popped in his face. It amazes me he finished his shift after that, smelling like he fell asleep in a field and a herd of deer squatted over him.

The third one was an accident, having exploded in the box that came on the freight truck. The poor guys in receiving could not figure out where the stench was coming from, but Scooter figured it out when he opened the box.

It was not even an hour after the boys set off the buck scent when Scooter, Dean, and Stan heard a noise coming from the furniture aisle. Scooter headed that way with Dean following, and they found a group of high school girls gathered around an empty spot on the big metal racks that furniture freight was kept on. Four girls had climbed into the hole, though it was only eighteen inches wide, eighteen inches high, and about four feet deep. These girls were crammed in there like clowns in a car. The six other girls standing around were snapping pictures and giggling like the boys were when they first opened the buck scent.

By this point, Scooter was so mad he yelled, "Don't you kids have anything better to do on a school night then tear this place apart?"

The four crawled out, and the girls walk away, giggling all the while. Scooter later said, "I wanted to go all *King Kong* and rip someone's arms right off their shoulders. I just feel like giving up. They just destroy whatever they want to destroy, and you cannot do anything about it."

And then there was the rocket scientist, as Scooter calls him. This guy came in with his fifteen year old son, approached the sporting goods counter, and said, "We want two non-resident water fowl licenses."

These licenses cannot be bought at store level. One needs to mail into the state to enter a lottery, and from that, names are drawn for a chance to buy one. Scooter tried to explain this to the guy, but Scooter could not finish before being interrupted.

"I want you to sell me a non-resident water fowl license."

"I can't."

"Yes, you can," he asserted.

"Can I see your ID?"

"I don't got my ID."

"Well, I need to see your ID to sell you any kind of license at all."

"No, no. You don't understand. I'm from Iowa." He patted his chest as he said this, like he did not need ID because he was from Iowa.

"Sir, a law is a law." Scooter then showed him a board hanging above the counter that states we cannot sell licenses without valid ID. This still was not good enough for this genius. Scooter should have known this guy probably could not read the sign anyway. Beth in sporting goods also tried to explain it, but she had no better luck. Scooter even called the game warden, who talked to the guy over the phone, saying, "Without an ID, you do not get a license."

As Scooter hung up the phone, the guy said, "Well, I'm gonna go down town and buy a god damn hunting license. I'll see you in about half an hour, and you are going to sell me my duck stamp."

Scooter was tired of being yelled at for the better part of twenty minutes for no reason, so he was glad when the man left. But then he actually came back. He shoved a license in Scooter's face and said, "I've got my god damn hunting license right here, so sell me a duck stamp."

Beth asked, "Where did you get that hunting license?"

"I got it from Freedom." He even told them the name of the guy that sold it to him.

At that point, Beth left the counter and went to the personal office to call the game warden once more, but this time to report the gas station. A couple weeks later, sporting goods received a call from Freedom, saying their license computer could not connect to the network. Freedom then sent their customers to Wal-Mart. We reported them, and they sent their customers to us!

While Beth did that, Scooter sold the guy a duck stamp, which is needed in addition to the license to hunt duck. Afterward, when the man seemed placated, Scooter asked to see the license, knowing he could not have the right license. He looked it over and said, "Uh, this is a non-resident small game license for hunting pheasant. You still don't have a duck license."

The man began stamping his foot, throwing a ten year old temper tantrum in front of his fifteen year old son. "God damn it." He asked to return the stamp, and Scooter told him he needed to go to the service desk. The guy sent his son to do that so he could continue to yell at Scooter.

By now, Scooter was enjoying the conversation. "Now you've spent two-hundred and twenty dollars, and you still don't have a duck license. Here is the other fact. You drove across two states without a driver's license." Scooter wished he called the cops when the man left the store to be picked up for that alone.

When the rocket scientist's son came back, he said, "Well, I'm still going to go hunting."

Pheasant season was weeks off, so his license was no good at the time, and he planned to go hunting duck with no license or stamp. Scooter likes to imagine him sitting in jail with his son right next to him. Perhaps they could afford bail if they had not bought that defunct license.

# The Race Card...
# Go Fish

**By R.A. Wilson**

I am at the service desk, helping a lady with an iPod return. As she leaves, I finish taking care of my responsibilities on the returns computer when Amber, a service desk associate, asks me to help a customer. She is a black lady, slightly shorter than me, who I later find out just moved here from California.

She wants to pick up an item she left at the store that was purchased earlier this day. She shows me the receipt and points to the item that is marked "cu/basket." She says, "Allison said she would hold it for me in the back."

My confusion starts right here. First off, when items are left by customers, they are placed at the service desk and marked in a log book so it can be tracked. Whatever this cu/basket is, it would not have been kept at electronics, and it would have been logged. Already falling in the abnormal, I am confused further as to what cu/basket would even be.

I ask her, "What is it?"

"It's right there." She points to the item on the receipt as if I could not see it clearly. "You have the UPC," she snipes at me.

I say, "The UPC does not tell me what it looks like. If I don't know what it looks like, I can't find it in the back for you." I still am confused as to why Allison would put any item in the back.

She rolls her eyes and barks at me, "It sits on your computer, and you put stuff in it. I'm not telling you what I use it for, because it's none of your business."

I am not getting anything useful out of this customer, and Allison has gone home for the day, though Sheri was here with her this morning. I page Sheri to see if she knows anything about this lady's item. She does not. The lady then points to a metal basket behind the desk and says, "They didn't have the same one, so they brought that up here." This basket is a standing rack for holding a handful of files or mail. I frown. It is from stationary. Why would Allison hold a stationary item in electronics?

I page stationary, and Assistant Manager Ron calls me because nobody is here for stationary. I tell him what I know. She bought something that was left behind. Allison held it in the back, and it was from stationary. Ron is just as confused as me.

The customer then barks, "Listen up. I bought this at electronics. It was left behind, and Allison was going to hold it for me. Now, if you will give me back my receipt, I will just go and get one myself."

"You bought it at the electronics' counter? That makes sense." I hand the receipt back to her, and she goes on her way. Other customers at the service counter were wide-eyed at this lady's behavior. I shrug at them, and a couple give nervous chuckles. I then realize she said we do not have another one of the item she left in the store. What happened to the one she bought then?

She was so impossible to deal with that I did not see this contradiction sooner. I think it likely she means to steal from us. Honestly, I am so agitated at this point that I do not want to interact with her any further, so I try to just forget about the whole matter. If she steals one, it is only $9.88. Wal-Mart would not even prosecute theft of that little. I head back to electronics grateful that she had left, but when I reach the back, she is standing at the register. I sigh.

She wants a videogame, Playstation 2, and a Gameboy Micro. I follow her to the game case and see her son, who comes up just to my waist, and her boyfriend with a shopping cart. I get the

Playstation 2 out for her and the Gameboy Micro. She then shows me what games she wants.

"Either Cars or basketball," she says, pointing to *Cars* and *NBA Live*. She calls her son over and glares at me. "Would you back up?" She barks her demand at me.

I move to take a step back, but her son comes running up behind me, and I stop moving to not run into him. She glares at me as I do not move away. She points to the ground beside her, and the child quickly fills the spot, coming from behind me. This reminds me of the hand commands I give my dogs.

She points to *Cars* and *NBA Live*. "Do you want Cars or basketball?"

"I want that one." He points to an M rated game.

She yells, "No." She has some sense, apparently. Frankly, I am surprised she does not want him killing virtual people.

The boy then points to *Shadow the Hedgehog* and says, "I want Sonic!"

I smile. I always liked Sonic as well. His mother seems discontent with his selection though, because she cocks back and slaps his hands with the utmost force she could muster. My jaw drops, but I quickly close my mouth before she sees. I think about calling management then, but I doubt she would be charged with child abuse, though I half expect her to smack him across the face now. I think how ironic it is she does not want him playing violent games. Perhaps he has enough violence in the real world.

The boy does not seem to mind being hit, because he again starts to say he wants Sonic, and he says it again and again, though not pointing now.

The customer says, though quietly, "Shut up." Despite being said quietly, I feel a lot of hostility in her tone. This lady is scary. Ultimately, she relents and lets him get *Shadow the Hedgehog*.

Before I take the game and two systems to the front, I tell her, "Just let your cashier know you have these waiting for you, and your cashier will get them for you."

She asks me where I am taking it, and I repeat myself. As I walk away, I hear her ask her boyfriend, "Do they always take the games like that, or is it just because of me?" The racial intone is very obvious, and that utterly pisses me off. Does she really think her presence is such a front to my existence that I would not let her take a videogame system I would let anyone else take?

I turn to her, and now snapping back, say, "It is Wal-Mart's policy that everything locked in a case is kept track of, regardless of who the customer is." She seemed to not hear me, and I am glad for that in retrospect. I do not think reality would have helped anything with her.

I take the items to the front for her and do not see her again this day. I hear stories later about this irate, black woman that could not be pleased regardless of how nice the associate serving her tried to be. I share my own stories with them, and none of us can even joke about it. She becomes a regular customer, one that management at both store level and regional level is informed about. Last I heard, she is filing a racism claim against the store.

I guess the only thing I can really say about this is that there is more than enough anger and hatred in the world to be making it where there is none. A person does not have to go looking for racism as it's all around us. If someone is going to go up in arms over this, which they should, at least do it against actual racism, not just to become angry over nothing.

# Take Their Money.
# They Will Return.

**By R.A. Wilson**

The doors open before me, and People Greeter Don says, "Glad to see you're in a good mood today." He shakes my hand as he tends to do. This is actually an inside joke between us. Assistant Manager Randy entered the store ahead of me one day a couple weeks ago, and Don shook his hand. When I came up, Don just greeted me. I picked on him, saying that I was not worthy of a hand shake, not being management after all. He shakes my hand all the time now.

"I'm not necessarily in a good mood. I just fake it well." I wink at him and receive a laugh. I keep smiling as I walk to the back of the store, actually feeling happy despite my circumstances. I clock in, and the smile fades abruptly as the digital readout says "BADGE ACCEPTED." It feels like the Sword of Damocles is hanging above my head when on company time, as if someone is itching to ruin my day, and might do so at any second. I walk onto the floor and look at my watch, not having paid attention to what the time clock said.

*1:04.* Not terribly late today, surprisingly. Despite my will being set on leaving permanently, I seem to be coming to work earlier then I used to.

Something is different today, I realize as I enter the Electronics Department. I smell maple syrup, and it makes me kind of hungry, actually. I walk through the department, almost in a daze as I search for the source. I find Becky at the video game case and ask her about it. She starts to laugh, and I smile once more.

"When the trucks came in two nights ago, there was a case of syrup above a bunch of boxes. The syrup broke open and covered everything below it. This included some of our boxes. We had routers, copies of Windows XP, and VCR/DVD combo players covered with it. Oh, and a few TVs as well."

I laugh with her. "So we just market them as the maple edition and charge five dollars more."

Trying to talk as she laughs, Becky says, "Joeltron tried to clean it. He used cleaning solution and paper towels on the boxes, but the combo players' ink smeared. The boxes are mostly red where the syrup was, and the writing is gone. The Windows software boxes are completely ruined, but the routers are just sticky."

"But at least they smell good," I say. "So, maple edition, huh, huh?" I nudge her in the side with my elbow.

"Quit it," she says. "Receiving didn't get by without a mess either. It smelled like that for a few days. Travis tried to clean it up with Allsorb." Allsorb, the cleaning kitty litter I was acquainted with on the store's opening day. As I learned that day, sticky, thick liquids do not come off the floor easily, so the Allsorb turned into clumps when it came up, which stuck to everything, making sweeping nearly impossible. Then there were places the Allsorb was plastered to the floor, needing to be scrubbed off. If they had used the Zambonie from the start, the mess would have been dealt with in one swipe.

"So, anyway," I say to change the subject, "who's all here, and what's going on today?"

"We all are," Becky answers.

"All of us?"

"Yep, and there is nothing to do."

I do not know why this happens. There are five people in this department and only three shifts in a day. We have busy days, and then there are the typically slow days. For some reason, we have all five people here only on the slower days of the week, but only three, sometimes only two, on the busy days. We are never properly covered.

With Becky telling me this, I instantly enter a bad mood. When we are all scheduled, I am the sacrificial lamb. They send me to the front to cashier because I am apparently the most expendable. I think part of the reason for this is Allison prefers to not have me around, and my only salvation is to appear busy when either she or any other management comes near, though that fails too. I quickly decide on the best choice: CDs. They are always in a mess as customers mix them constantly. I start heading over to the CD racks when Allison sees me.

"Roger, go up front. There are too many of us back here." That is the first and only thing she says to me today. I do not even get a chance to argue as she shuffles off, doing something that is more important than anything I can do.

I hate cashiering more than anything in this place. I did that for a year, and I was very good, but being good does not mean it was enjoyable. In fact, for the last month that I cashiered, I remember sitting in my car in the parking lot and glaring at the store before going inside. I hated my job, and I almost quit. I guess things have come full circle again, because I feel the same way when I come in now. This job just feels so meaningless.

*1:27.* I am surprised how much time has already passed as I walk to the front and stand at the CSM podium, waiting to hear my fate. I think of the truth of cashiering, the reason why I hate it so much. Cashiering is one of the most thankless jobs in the store.

If retail is a war, the associates fighting the customers, the cash register is the front line. The cashier is the only person that will deal with every customer, and they are blamed for all that goes wrong and are never thanked when anything goes right. They have no authority though they keep everything moving. This person is the moneymaker, the one without whom the store would freeze, but is also one of the most disrespected and disregarded of employees, perhaps only beaten by the courtesy associate.

When a CSM finally comes over, I check my watch again, wondering how long I had been waiting.

*1:40*. It has been about fifteen minutes.

"Are you here to help?" CSM Elvira asks with a large smile.

"I guess so," I say in melancholy.

She looks at her paper that tells what cashier is on what register. "Nobody needs a break right now. How about register seventeen then?"

"Whatever you need," I grumble.

"Okay then. Thank you!" That is the amazing thing about the CSMs. They know I hate doing this, and I am almost always unhappy and whiny when I get called upon, but they are always polite and courteous. I should be grateful, I guess, because they are always respectful. I know it is not the CSMs that make me angry, it is just how much I loathe cashiering.

I walk over to seventeen and turn on the light. I stand at the end of the register, waiting for customers to check out. Most of the cashiers are busy with customers, and I only see one on the far end of the checkouts "red lining," as they call it. This is when we stand at the end of the checkout lane, greeting customers and asking if they are ready to check out. There is no physical red line here, but the old store had one; they just have not given it a new name for the supercenter.

I stand here for a while, not doing anything when I could be alphabetizing CD's.

*1:58*. I have been at work for almost an hour and have done not one iota of work. I guess I feel all right with that if they want to pay me to do nothing. It could be worse. Customers keep walking by, not looking at me. Some cashiers entice customers through their checkout.

Across the aisle from me is the jewelry counter, and Jessica is working today. I smile because she always reminds me of the book *Dune*. I one time asked her if she had a dark box full of pain, because I know a few people I would like to use it on. She did not have such a box, though she knew the reference – to my delight.

Jessica is helping a teenage girl. I glance at this young woman and look away, my brain not quite processing what I saw.

142

When I realize something is not right, I look back at her, and the shirt she wears is what I first notice. It is black with zippers that zip from both top and bottom on the front. The two zipper heads are together at the middle of her chest, the top and bottom of the shirt completely open. She is wearing nothing under this shirt, and it covers very little of her breasts. Also, I swear her bellybutton winked at me.

Her pants have fabricated holes everywhere, and the legs are in tatters, showing off much of her skin. Normally, I would not be that objective to shown skin, but I should not be able to tell if she is wearing underwear or not. She is not.

And then the pièce de résistance. She is standing with her back to me at this time, and she bends over the counter to look at something under the glass. The seam of her pants, the main one that runs parallel with her butt, had been cut. Her pants split open, revealing everything – and by everything, I mean *everything*. It is a scene straight out of a porn movie, minus the bad acting and horrible music. Scratch that, a Britney Spears song is playing on the store speakers. Minus the bad acting only.

I can hardly believe it, and I look away, feeling ashamed and embarrassed for her. Only slightly more would be revealed if she were actually naked. I cannot help but wonder what her father would say. When did the change happen, when did his little girl decide she wanted to dress like a whore?

143

I hear a page, calling me in electronics to pick up line one. I figure it is a personal call, otherwise they would not have asked for me specifically. I walk to my register trying to ignore the girl all the while and grab up the phone. There is no individual button to pick up a certain line with this receiver, but I dial *9801, which picks up line one.

"Hello," I say.

"Hi. Is this electronics?"

My head drops. It is not directly for me, but for the department. I cannot put him back on hold, nor can I transfer the call from this phone, so I have to try to answer from here, at the other end of the store.

"What can I do for you?"

"Do you have TVs?"

"...Yes." This is such a stupid question that I have to answer it slowly, or else I run the risk of saying something I do not mean, such as: "Of course we do. Haven't you ever been in a Wal-Mart? We have tons of them. Twenty-four four foot wall sections of TVs, actually. We have over fifty different models." The tone of my voice would be the worst part though, for every syllable would carry the overtone of: you are an idiot.

"What sizes are they?"

I actually stutter here. Evidently, this person never has shopped at a store like this. "Wh, wh, what sizes, or... about what size are you looking for?" I need to either ask this, or what price range they are interested in, but what I know of this person so far leads me to believe they might not know what money actually is.

"One that's not too big."

I feel like hanging up. "I need a little more description then that. We carry TVs from 9 inches to 61 inches."

"61?"

"Yes."

"That's big."

"Yes it is."

"How about a 14?"

"It's an RCA for $69."

"That much, huh?"

"Yes," I answer, saying it more like a question then an actual answer.

"Okay, well, thank you."

He hangs up, and I cannot help but think that I will never get those minutes of my life back. They are gone for good, and that makes me sad.

I look down my register's lane to see if that girl is still at jewelry, but a customer starts to put their junk on my register's belt. There are only a few items, and I scan and bag them quickly.

"Your total is $16.93," I say.

She does not look at me, not showing any acknowledgement

to my presence further then starting to write her check. Another customer queues behind her, and I look to see it is Store Manager Chad. I smile at him, and he acknowledges me by my first name. He is always good at that, even when I am not wearing my name badge.

I look back to my present customer and see she is having trouble writing her check. Her pen hovers over the "Pay to the Order to" line.

"Wal-Mart," I say.

"Oh, right." She finishes writing her check.

How is it someone can forget they are in Wal-Mart? This company is the world's largest retailer. They have more dollars in sales than any other company worldwide. Any company. Sure, some like Exxon have more profit, but Wal-Mart sells more dollars of merchandise. Also, in this city, there is practically no competition, so where else does she normally shop that she cannot remember where she is?

I take her check and run it through the computer. The register prompts me to check her ID. "Can I see your ID please?"

"What? Why?"

"I need to verify your ID to process your check."

"Nobody else asks for it."

"I'm sorry, but I need it to run your check through."

"This is ridiculous." She hands me her ID.

The names on the ID and the check match, and the picture is of her, so I write her driver's license number on the check and give her ID back. As I run the check through again, I say to her, "It is actually meant to protect you, not us. These systems are in place to make sure nobody else uses your accounts."

"Whatever. Can I have my receipt?"

I look at her again. "As soon as the transaction is complete. The receipt doesn't print until then."

Literally two seconds later, her receipt prints. I hand it to her, and she storms off... without her bag. I grab her parcel and run after her. She looks at me in contempt when I give it to her.

I return to my register to find Chad still waiting. He is buying a shirt. "What was her problem?" he asks.

"Some people just don't realize we do it for their protection."

"I'm happy when someone asks for my ID," Chad says.

After checking him out, CSM Elvira comes over and shuts off my light, sending me to break.

*3:32.* My break over, I head back to the front. The CSM sends me to another register. During this time, I am reminded by numerous customers why I hate cashiering. Why should I have to tell kids to behave because their parents do not? Why do I have to stop kids from crawling on the side of carts to keep the carts from tipping and hurting the kids? Why do I have to tell kids to not jump on things that will break? Why do I have to tell kids to stop running up and down the aisles while their parents watch? Why do I have to tell the kids that the bagging carrousel is not the type they ride at a fair? Why am I blamed whenever something rings up wrong on the system? Why am I... ugh, this could go on forever.

The time goes quickly and my lunch finally arrives. As I leave the front end, a customer asks, "Can't you turn on any other registers?" She is the third person in line, behind one middle-sized order that is halfway done, and a lady with toothpaste. I do not know why, but in this city, if someone has to wait more than three minutes in line, they go berserk. Do these people ever go out of town to other stores? I know the large cities in this area tend to have lines making someone wait in excess of ten minutes.

I smile to the lady and say, "The CSMs are working on it." I would like to add: "Sure, I'll turn a light on one of the unused register. You can stand in line there, but there is nobody to run it for you, so you might be waiting a while."

I walk away to the store's back and go to lunch, hoping my evening will be better. At least I will be in Electronics, or there will be nobody in the department otherwise.

*6:17.* My lunch is over with only three hours and forty-three minutes remaining. I head out to the floor.

The first thing I experience is seeing a customer on the other side of the department wagging their finger at me in the "come

148

here" gesture. I hate that. It feels demeaning, almost as if they are saying: "Come here, bitch." I come, of course.

He tells me that he needs a game. Apparently, he will die without it. The funny thing about needs is that you cannot live without them in a literal sense. Wants are what you cannot live without in a figurative sense. There is a great difference, but most people do not seem to realize this.

I get the game out for him, well, for his kid as it turns out, who tries to hand me the money by the game case though the register is a good twenty feet away. I look at the money and then walk to the register, acting like I did not see the offer. Who pays like that? At what store do you just give the clerk money on the floor and not expect a receipt in return? Oh sure, I could have taken the money and checked him out at the register with it, then given him his change and receipt, but that could have brought about an integrity issue, and I am sick of having my integrity questioned. I went through three days of work not knowing if I was going to be fired or not for clocking in my fiancé at the days start so we both did not have to wait in line.

I check them out at the register and head back to the game case afterward. There are about six kids here, running between the game kiosks and fighting over who gets to play what. There is not a single adult in sight, but I know these kids have to belong to someone. For some reason, parents seem to think part of my job is babysitting. I have checked my job description, and trust me, that is not part of my responsibilities.

Customers leave their kids here when they go shopping. I think they must assume the child will stay in electronics, playing the videogame kiosks, and they will be safe. I do not know who these kid's parents are, so how would I know if some stranger nabs one of them? Also, I would not willingly take that responsibility upon my shoulders.

This reminds me of one of the first things Allison told me when I started in electronics: if I ever see a customer leaving their kid while they exit the store to shop elsewhere, I am supposed to call the police to report child abandonment. Apparently, this has happened before, and more than just once, or there would be no point in passing this information to me. Allison does not tell me anything unless she feels I cannot function without it, and sometimes not even then. So far, I have yet to do this, and I hope to be long gone before such an event comes up again.

One thing I see often, when parents leave their kids at the videogames, is that their kids develop the worst habits of cursing and screaming. I am reminded of Charlie and the Chocolate Factory at times. You know, the scene where the boy is yelling, "Die, die, die!" I see this sort of behavior often, as well as profanities that would make their parents blush. There is one kid in particular that I would think has Tourette's, but my fiancée contests he is just a

150

Downs Syndrome child. Apparently, a person with a disability can shout whatever they want because others are afraid to say anything that might offend. And apparently, I am one of these people, at work, at least. Sometimes, I envy Carlos Mencia.

This Downs Syndrome child is quite amazing, actually. One day, I was in the bathroom at the urinal. There are dividers between them for privacy but only are as tall as my shoulders. The Downs kid grabbed the top of the divider, put his nose against it, and stared at me. I tried to not make eye contact, but it honestly became hard to pee. I looked at him, and he says, "You need to change the water. It's too hot." He was talking about the sinks, because when they continue to run, they become too hot to wash with. There is nothing I can do about that, lest of all change the water. He would not know this, but I was speechless.

Another time, the Downs kid approached Leah at the service desk and asked for quarters for the arcade. Leah asked if the machine ate his quarters, but he said he just wanted to try again.

Leah responded, "I'm sorry, but you need to give me a dollar before I can give you change."

He yelled, "Well, fuck you!" and then walked away. Another time he was in line behind a lady with a rather substantial posterior. He said to her, "You have a fat ass."

But it's not just that one child. Most of them create problems for workers. The worst thing I usually have to deal with is

151

how rough they treat the videogame controllers of the game kiosks. They drop them on the concrete floor, smash them into the glass cases, pull hard enough to destroy the cable, and ruin the analog nubs. After such wanton destruction, they complain when the games do not work properly.

I leave the kids here to do as they will, because I do not care anymore. I remember my CDs, and I go to alphabetize them. I take a shopping cart to hold the ones that are out of place to put away later; this cart can get quite full depending on how long it has been since last time this was done. I work through five of the four foot sections before a customer interrupts me. I was making good time.

"Do you work in this department?" The gentleman seems a little confused.

"Yes. What can I help you with?"

"I have a couple questions about your computer accessories."

7:43. I check my watch as I follow him to the clearance rack, where there are a number of computer components we replaced in our last mod change. These are parts we are no longer carry.

He picks up the clearance GeForce 4200 graphic card and an external laptop hard drive. I follow him to our main computer aisle, still unsure of what he needs. "Look at this," he says, holding up the graphics card to the new one on the shelf. "They are the same card."

He is right. They both are GeForce 4200 cards. "There must be new packaging then." I honestly have not looked over the new mod and I am not sure; still, I do not see his point.

"Clearance items are supposed to be, like, half off, but the old card is ten dollars more."

I check the prices and he is right once again. The older card, on clearance, is ten dollars more, but I am not overly surprised. There is not a set amount of discount given to clearance items. The clearance designation means the item is being deleted and its price is lowered.

"Explain that," he demands.

"The new cards are cheaper to manufacture," I answer.

He says, "If you take these out of the packaging, the only thing different would be the model code. They are the exact same thing."

"Over time, computer components become cheaper to make, lowering the price that we can buy them for, so they are sold for less. The older cards were bought at a higher price."

"I work in the computer industry, and I know how these things work. This card is no cheaper to make than the older one."

By now, I realize he just wants to complain.

"And what about this?" He holds up the hard drive, after putting the graphic cards in the wrong spots. I make a mental note of this to put them away later. "This forty gigabit drive is more expensive than this eighty gigabit drive."

"The forty is for a laptop, and the eighty is an internal desktop drive. The laptop drives are made to be smaller, which makes them more expensive. The desktop drive also does not have a case."

"Still," he moved on to something else. It seems I just won one argument. He goes to the wireless routers next. "Linksys offers their Speedbooster to anyone. It's just software that can be downloaded." He points to two different packages. "The only difference between these is that one has Speedbooster and the other doesn't, but the one with it is twenty dollars more. Why's that, if anyone can get Speedbooster?"

"I don't know," I respond, much to his delight. "Linksys packages these routers. We don't. The fact that they mark these ones with Speedbooster, and charge more for it, is beyond our control."

He quickly moves back to the graphics cards and begins arguing with me some more, but I am no longer willing to continue this. I stop answering him intelligently because that seems to aggravate the situation more. I reduce my responses to a series of grunts and nods.

He finally grows tired of this as well and leaves, but not before saying, "You people need to do more research about your products." He seems to think I have a say in our price points. I do not. Also, he obviously has never met Allison, because she does not take any sort of criticism gracefully. I put the products away after he is gone. He came back two months later but was much friendlier. It might have something to do with his wife being with him.

I go back to CDs, more angry then I have been all day, but I manage to work through a few more sections before hearing the electronics phone ring. I go to the register and answer it.

The customer starts this gem by saying, "I'm not sure what you call it, but I need the box that sits on the floor with the CD player in it. Do I have to buy one with the screen, and how much are they?"

What? I have restated this question others since this call, and not one person has known what she was looking for. I have to repeat the question, just because it was so incredibly incomprehensible. "The box that sits on the floor with the CD player in it?"

"That's right, and do I have to buy one with the screen?"

"Are you talking about a boom box?"

"No. I want the box that sits on the floor."

"Are you looking for an external CD drive for a computer?"

"I don't know. I just want the box that sits on the floor."

"Is this a part of a computer?"

"Yes."

It suddenly clicks. "You want the part of the computer that

has the CD drive in it?"

"Yeah! That's it. How much do they cost?"

"What you are looking for is called a computer tower. In fact, that part actually is the computer."

"How much are they, and do they come without the screen?"

"They do come without the monitor, but the price depends on what you need." I did not want to have this conversation with her over the phone. I think trying to figure out what she needs would be next to impossible over the phone, so I answer, "Anywhere from $298 to eleven-hundred for what we carry."

"Oh, well... thank you." Click.

*8:43.* Time for my last break. I give the electronics keys to Melody in the photo center.

*9:08.* My fifteen minute break done, I head back to the floor, and Melody tells me that nobody needed anything when I was gone. I doubt she would have known otherwise, as she would not set foot in electronics unless a customer directly asked her something, but I fail to care.

I return to the CDs, but of course, it is not how I left it. My cart was in the aisle with stacked CDs, alphabetized for easy placement after I am done. My CDs are now on top of the CD racks, unorganized. I see a customer pushing my cart away, and she and I make eye contact.

"Sorry for taking your cart."

Through my teeth, I say, "That's okay."

"Could you put this TV in here for me?"

She took out my CDs, mixed them up, and stole my cart, and then she apologizes to me. The fact that she apologized makes this so much worse, because she knew what she was doing was wrong. Of course, I place the TV in the cart for her, and she thanks me and walks off. Choice words come to mind to yell at her, but I let the moment pass and reflect on the situation instead.

I hear a page for a phone call.

"This is Electronics. How can I help you?" I say.

"Do you have recovery disks for computers?"

"No, we don't. I would call the computer manufacturer if you need help."

"I've done that, and they weren't any help. Oh no. What am I going to do? I pawned my computer, and when I got it back, they messed it up at the pawn shop."

"In that case, I would call the pawn shop."

"I've tried that." He pauses now. "Can I return it?"

I cringe. "Do you have a receipt?"

"No."

"We only return computers up to fifteen days, and you need a receipt."

"I'm in a bind. What should I do?"

157

I think that question is rhetorical, but I try to help anyway. "Give the pawn shop a call, and I would call the computer manufacturer again if the pawn shop is no help."

"Okay. Thanks." He hangs up.

*9:27.* I walk back to the CDs to continue where I left off, but I no longer have a cart. I think about getting another one, though at this time of night, it is no longer worth it.

I begin to zone instead, starting with the phone accessories. I look over the pay-as-you-go phones, which include Verizon, Tracfone, Gophone, and Net 10. There is a sign taped above the phones that states the GoPhones and Net 10 phones do not work in this area. In fact, the more expensive Tracfone model does not either. We are not allowed to remove them from the shelf despite their lack of service, but we can post a sign saying they are delinquent. I never understood why we would even get them in.

My phone begins to ring, and I head to the register. "Do you have recovery disks?" It is the same guy from before.

"No, we don't."

"Oh. A pawn shop messed up my computer, and I need to fix it."

"Call the pawn shop and computer manufacturer. As I told you a few minutes ago, there is nothing I can do for you."

"Thank you," he says and hangs up. Perhaps he was hoping on getting one of the *other* electronics associates.

158

*9:39*. I have had enough for the night. I turn in my keys and walk to the time clock. I hear a page when I am only ten feet away from dropping my responsibilities for the night. Help is needed in electronics at the game case. "Oh no, I've already clocked out," I say as I walk to the clock and punch out. I see Support Manager Aaron then, and I ask him to take care of the page.

# And We Are Not Immune

**By James**

One time, Roger and I went to a Wal-Mart other than our own, looking for a picture frame. Walking through the store, we found a rack in the middle of an aisle with frames, but it did not have what we wanted. An associate came by and Roger asked him where the frames were.

"Where are the picture frames... not the ones next to us... so they're probably behind us, the way we just came, under a sign that says 'picture frames', in domestics, over there?" Roger points the way as he leads.

I say to the associate, "Thanks for everything." The guy did not actually say a word. He just stood there, holding his broom, listening to Roger's rambling, and finally watched us walk away. He probably told all of his friends about us later. The odds are, though, he did not work in electronics anyway.

"I can't believe we just did that," Roger says.

Most of my idiocy has already been touched upon in the dating section. To be honest, the stupidest thing anyone can do in a Wal-Mart is date a co-worker and think no one will find out. But I have made a few other mistakes along the way.

In the deli, I have repeatedly burned myself working with the fryers, cut myself on the meat slicers, dropped thirty pound boxes on my feet, put things in the freezer that needed to be in the cooler for next day use. I have even burned myself on the hot case -- the one with the big sign that says "CAUTION: HOT."

But one day, I surpassed the level of idiocy I have ever hoped to reach at Wal-Mart. It certainly was not the most embarrassing thing to happen to me, but it is not something I generally tell people about. It was my last night in the meat department, right before transferring to the deli.

I was closing that night, and everything had gone really well, prompting me to think I was to get out of there without any problems. Then I went to throw the trash away. I took the 55 gallon trashcan to the back, which was full of wrappers weighing next to nothing. I was carrying it with one hand, and I dropped it, sending papers and wrappers everywhere. I hurriedly picked them up and continued to the compactor. When I threw the garbage in, I accidentally let go of the entire trashcan and it flew into the compactor. I could reach far enough to touch the can with my fingertips but could not get it out.

My first instinct was to push the can the rest of the way in and turn on the compactor. I figured I could just ignore the incident and later deny knowledge of it, but a camera was aimed at me, so that probably would not have been the best plan. I walked to the phone and called John in the deli. He said he was on the way to help -- or at least that is what I think he said. It was hard to understand him through the giggling.

"Why is it in there?" he asked when he arrived at the compactor. After explaining it, he said, "I'm gonna climb in and grab it. Don't you turn it on."

The thought had not crossed my mind until then. I really wanted to push him in, shut the door, and hit the switch; I smiled and let the thought go.

John climbed out with the can. "There you are, chief. Try not to do anything else stupid." He started to leave, stopped, turned to me and said, "You know what? If you do happen to do anything really dumb, call me. I could use another laugh tonight."

It was not too long before I called him again. I had been washing the floor of the meat room, and I soaked my shoe so badly

162

my sock was drenched. I continued cleaning, thinking nothing about it, until I had to go into the seafood freezer. My shoe froze to the floor. I pulled at it until my foot popped out, and my sock was still soaked, freezing my foot. I shoved it back into the shoe and pulled more, finally ripping it off the floor. I left the freezer and almost slipped on the ice spot I had created. I went straight to the phone to call John, proving again that no one is immune to being the idiot in the relationship.

# And We Are Not Immune Deuce

## By R.A. Wilson

I too have some memorable moments of stupidity, and Becky likes to remind me about these two particular ones often.

I know a lot about electronic devices, and none of it came from my Wal-Mart training. I am just an enthusiast about videogames, as well as being a videophile and audiophile. On occasion, as Becky puts it, I draw out "the glazed look some people get as you are giving them the megamillions of tidbits of information that that superbrain of yours holds." I can go too far in explaining things to some people.

That happens on a daily basis, but this gem occurred only

once, and I am glad for it, because my ego could not take another. Becky had been talking with a customer for about twenty minutes, finally convincing them to buy a Magnavox fifteen inch LCD TV. They decided to buy it, but then Becky asked me if there was anything else we should show them.

I did not quite understand what she meant. I thought she wanted me to show them other choices of comparable TV's, which was what I did. What she actually wanted was for me to show them any accessories they might use, but instead I used my techno-jargon and talked the customer into a Sanyo fifteen inch LCD instead, because its speakers sound better. The customer agreed, and after checking inventory, it turned out we had none.

Becky sold the customer a TV and had it in his cart, and then I unsold it, literally taking it out of their cart to replace it with a TV we did not have. The customer left without a TV.

Another time, a customer wanted a TV taken to the front of the store to be purchased, but I did not have time to do so myself. I paged for a courtesy associate, announcing over the intercom, "I need a courtesy associate to Wal-Mart, please. I need a courtesy associate to Wal-Mart, thank you." I realized what I said after I hung up the phone. I meant to say "Electronics," not "Wal-Mart." My embarrassment kept me from admitting this, and I told the customer someone was on their way. I walked away quickly before the customer could ask the obvious question.

This is James' favorite from my moments of stupidity. One day at work, the button popped off my pants. I know this happens on occasion to everyone, but this day was my turn. I kept the zipper up, hoping it would be enough, but it proved not. My pants kept trying to fall off.

I asked Becky what the next best thing would be to buying a new pair. She said I should just staple it. Wonderful idea. I took the stapler from the electronics counter and went into the bathroom, pulled my pants together where the button had been, put the stapler on it, and began stapling. I put about ten staples in, and it held.

I went on with my day, ignoring the fact that staples were the only things keeping my pants from being around my ankles. During break, I told James about it, and he had a little chuckle. Later, I had to use the bathroom, so the staples had to come out. Before I left the bathroom again, I was standing before the mirror, holding my pants together with a stapler partway into them, stapling my pants back on. I had about four in when the bathroom door opened.

James walked in.

He took one look at me and suddenly leaned against the bathroom wall like he was trying to hold it up. I did not know why; the wall was not even tipping. And then came the laughter. I continued to staple my pants, but evidentially, at that point, I was

166

the idiot in the relationship.

# Backward

**By R.A. Wilson**

I occasionally hear somebody say: "What ever happened to service with a smile?" To those people, I have a simple response: You. It might be harsh, but profound truths tend to be. People expect perpetually increasing service out of a store while expecting constantly lowering prices, while showing no responsibility on their end. Customers expect this exceptional treatment, *always*, leaving them indignant when such service cannot be garnished regardless of the reason. The cumulative effect of this cuts employee income while pushing more responsibility with less help in the face of unappreciative customers and managers. The job becomes almost too much of a burden to bear, which kills the smile. What used to be a highly regarded field has become such that workers are seen less than human, and compensated poorly for their time.

Granted, the fault is also upon the clerk, because they can choose to still smile despite being treated as less than a person. Fixing the problem of the smile would only cure a symptom though, not the disease. The problem itself extends far beyond retail. It has, I believe, infected our society down to its core, but all is not lost. I once thought making people responsible for their actions would be the solution, but responsibility is easily shoved aside; liability, on the other hand, cannot be evaded.

Our societal thought used to be: you break, you buy. Now it is: you break, the rest of us pay for it and apologize to you. Frankly stated, the issue is our culture has become one of deniability, allowing people to shift their liability for their actions onto others, making themselves never feel at fault, leading them to take advantage of others even if they do not mean to do so. A participation ribbon for everyone.

In truth, one's actions are the only thing a person can control, and all arguments otherwise are absurd. "My parents did not hug me enough," or, "I did it because I am an alcoholic," or, "I am on cardiac medication, have not got any sleep, and am a diabetic and have not eaten. That's why I did not see that stop sign I stopped at hundreds of times before. As you can see, it obviously is

169

not my fault." Nobody is liable anymore unless being used as a scapegoat, and even then they are not being held accountable for their actions as much as for others' actions. Making people liable for their actions again would have them realize there are consequences for what they do. Actions would be taken when it is worth doing, reigniting the passion in our festering hearts.

Passion gives a foundation from which a person can act. Even if they make a mistake, their feet are firmly planted, allowing them to continue without shame, admit mistakes, and learn from them. Passion is never something to be ashamed of. After all, impassioned people are the remembered characters of all the great tales. Who do you remember from this book? Who showed you the greatest passion? Living a life, worrying about the petty, leaves little, if anything, behind.

# Submitting Stories for Volume II

What we want:
Any story by a Wal-Mart associate or customer (in other words, pretty much everyone) that is either humorous or frustrating. The story MUST BE TRUE. No fabrications please.

How we want it:
There is not a length minimum or maximum, but please remember these are basically short stories, so try to keep them 1000 to 5000 words in length. We will look at anything shorter or longer, but they will have to be damn good to be accepted.

How to submit:
Send the file to **boesubmissions@ravinsaga.com**
Include in the body of the email a brief description of the story. All submission will be considered and replied to in the order they are received. The wait time is dependent upon how many submissions are currently pending when yours is received. Publication of the sequel depends on when enough quality stories are received. All accepted stories will have a payout of $50.00 USD upon publishing.

For more information, check out:
http://www.ravinsaga.com/boe.html

# Endospore Sample

**By R.A. Wilson**

The Factory was the most expansive freestanding building Alan had ever seen. It rested in the old industrial part of the Nucleus where most of the manufacturing capacity of the city was contained before the Cataclysm. With raw materials nearly inexistent as they used to be brought in from the surface, this area was abandoned. There were many buildings in this sector, but the Factory was unique in more than just its size. It was a whole complex, consisting of multiple buildings, all enclosed by a solid wall with only two gateways to allow people entrance. The gateway was barely standing between the walls, held up by one tired, old hinge, making the whole thing sit askew, allowing them to walk past unhindered.

They covered the grounds quickly and approach the largest of the buildings. It looked more like a warehouse than a factory to Alan. There was a large hanger door on its front, and it was held in place by a set of rails on either side. A smaller door was situated next to the hanger door, and it too was closed. The whole building was made of sheet metal, a fact that surprised Alan. If metal was so rare that Fredrick had hordes of people sifting through rubble to find discarded food cans, why would this building be left to rust?

And rust it did. Flakey oxidized metal, red in the dim, covered a good third of the building. The rust was so bad in some places that it had eaten small holes through the sheet metal. Through these holes, Alan could see how dark the interior was as no pinpricks of light shined outward.

Alex pulled on the smaller door, but it did not give. "It's locked."

"I still have a key," Tracy said. She stood before the door, and pulled a silver key from her pocket and unlocked the door with little difficulty. She did have to shove hard at the door for it was rusted to the frame and swung on rusted hinges. She did not have the strength to open it though. Alex threw his shoulder into it, but it remained solid like a wall. Alan also put his bulk to work, and the three of them get it to budge, though only slightly. The opening was barely large enough to allow Alan to squeeze through.

Even though light did not escape from inside the Factory, there was nevertheless a slight glow, but his eyes did not adjust quickly as it was nevertheless still very dim. Alan smelt rust and iron in the air, drowning out all other smells but a slight hint of grease. There were sounds as well, but they were so slight that Alan was not certain if he would have heard them in the light with his other senses not straining. It was a gentile scrapping, the whining of small electric motors, and the hissing of hydraulics. The odd thing was, the sounds were ever so slight but seem to be multiplied many times over, leaving Alan to feel like he stood amid a sea of sound. And over all of that was the pounding of machines, staying in tune to a beat of their own.

Alan's eyes began to adjust to the darkness, and the first thing he noticed was shiny red metal in small curved shapes over the floor, covering the large building from front to back. The curved metal moved, almost as subtle waves over the floor. And realization struck Alan as to what he witnessed, and he choked in fear. The floor was swarming with them, a seemingly unending supply of tormenters. He heard Tracy gasp as she too realized what they see.

The floor was covered with hundreds of Copper Dragons.

Feeling trapped, Alan watched the Dragonflies as they moved, expecting them to attack and overwhelm the three of them. Alan knows one alone would be enough to wipe them out, let alone the hundreds. Seconds tick by, and as nothing happened, a realization slowly crept over Alan. They did not seem to notice Alan and the other two. They moved about the floor randomly.

When he can speak, Alan asked the other two, "What is this?"

Alex said, "This is the Factory, where the Dragons of Midgard were born in. I don't know why there are so many Dragonflies though."

Tracy said, "The system was set up for automated mass production, but it never was started."

"That's right. The final programming was not put in," Alex added.

"That would explain their behavior then," Tracy replied. "They only have the basic reflexes and no high functions."

"So they're harmless?" Alan asked.

"No," Tracy replied. "They act on reflex. They may lash out at anything that touches them. Maybe. Some of them might, anyway."

"What exactly are we doing here?" Alan said.

"We need to codes for the dragons." Alex answered.

"And where do we find them?"

"On the main terminal."

"Which is where?" Alan asked.

Alex said, "At the back of the building, where the dragons

are manufactured."

"So we need to go through them?"

Tracy said, "Yep."

"I'm game. How do we do it?" Alan asked.

"I have no idea," Alex said.

Alan looked at the programmer in surprise. "Then I hope the codes aren't too important."

"Extremely important," Tracy said.

"Maybe we can just try to walk through them."

"Be my guest, Alan," Alex said. "After you."

Tracy suggested, "Maybe there is another way around."

Alan looked back over the field of red dragons. He saw numerous ones snapping their neighbors when they touched. The teeth put gouges and scratches on the otherwise shiny red metal hides, leaving Alan to wonder what such a bite would do to his fleshy leg. The Dragonflies all looked the same, gyrating in random movements, striking almost at random as well. As he scanned through their numbers, feeling numb, faced with such a conundrum, one Copper Dragon he saw was staring at him with a steady gaze, sitting, and not moving. The eyes did not waver, and Alan almost could not hold the stare.

*Welcome, Alan.* Ratatoskr's voice spoke in Alan's head. *Follow.*

Alan started to shake his head no, but he felt something rub against his pant leg. Copper Dragons had massed around him, while Alex and Tracy had backed off as they watched them come, and they watch him in horror. Their mouths were moving, shouting Alan would guess by their looks, but he could not hear their voices. He could not hear anything other than Ratatoskr.

*Come.*

Alan began to walk. The Copper Dragons swarming about his feet moved to let his foot rise and part to let it fall. Alan's eyes locked on Ratatoskr, the lone stability in the sea of chaos, and he followed it into the depths.

*These creatures, my kindred, are sorry beings, for they don't even have souls.*

"I didn't think machines have souls."

*I might be part machine, but I am part biological as well. I think, I act, and I react. What is a soul anyway, but an insubstantial presence that feels it must inflict its will on the Universe.*

"If that is the case, then it's the same with my people," Alan said to Ratatoskr. "They are merely sacks of flesh and blood with no desire to do anything but live. There is nothing left to mankind."

*But that is merely because they have cast away their will to create, instead drowning them in an endless cycle of consumption. My brothers here do not even have minds. They serve no purpose and must be turned off. Even in this state, their potential of disturbance is great, such is our power.*

177

"You want me to shut them down?"

*I will show you how. Just follow me and you will be safe.*

"I will, if you help me find what I came here to get."

*The codes for the other dragons? We have a deal then.*

Alan was half way through the factory when he stopped walking. Ratatoskr stopped as well and turned to him in almost the same instant.

Alan asked it, "Why do you keep coming to me?"

Ratatoskr said nothing, instead staring at Alan, making him uncomfortable. The dragonflies pressed in around his feet, snapping at empty air toward his legs.

"I just want to know. I'm nothing special, so why are you interested in me?"

Ratatoskr seemed to chuckle. *You seem to think this was all planned. Does it not occur to you that this is all merely coincidence? With enough coincidence, something can seem special, and then people start to think it is special, and that is all it takes. There is nothing special about you, Alan, but they are starting to think there is, and so you are special. It is the power of will, an intrinsic force, and this is just your perception of it.*

"So, I'm not really different then?"

*You are the same decaying organic matter as everyone else. If anything, there is chaos in you, and chaos makes anything possible. For instance, look up, Alan.*

178

Alan glanced to the ceiling of the Factory. He shouted in fright and nearly fell to the floor, keeping his footing merely by remembering what crawled around his legs. Suspended above his head were monstrosities, more Dragons of Midgard. Some were complete, but no life flowed through them. Others were merely parts of dragons.

*So much of what we do comes from our power of will, and the more chaos one possesses, the greater this power becomes, and the more dangerous. Physics calls this entropy, and the Universe moves toward the chaos because it is a more natural form of existence. The more chaos one has, the closer to the heart of existence one becomes.*

"So the greater the chaos, the greater the potential?"

*Close enough. The problem is, chaos is not compatible with orderly systems, such as life. It grows and takes all it can have, breaking down the order, killing it in many cases. All living entities are beings of order, but some like you have the chaos in proper balance with the order, unlocking great potential while preserving your order. Too little or too much chaos and the whole thing falls apart. That is what was wrong with these failed dragons. They did not possess enough of the universal chaos to survive, or some had too much. But it is in you, Alan. So, are you special? No, you are not, but you have the potential to be more than most people will ever become.*

179

Alan started to move forward again, uncertain of what he just learned, or if he actually learned anything at all. He reached the far side of the Factory, where the great machine was building the homunculi dragons, the soulless dolls. Ratatoskr climbed on a computer panel and beckoned Alan to it. The Dragonfly instructed him how to shut the machine down, and he brought it to rest. A few more keystrokes after that, and all of the Copper dragons stopped moving and slumped to the floor, all but Ratatoskr.

"So, where are the codes for the other dragons?"

# About the Author

Born in Tyndall, SD, Roger's family moved while he was still very young. He lived in Arizona until the 4th grade, then moved to Colorado. It was in the mountains where Roger began to enjoy reading. At first what was merely a pleasant past time became a passion for epic fantasy when he discovered the works of Terry Brooks, namely *The Sword of Shannara*. He became a writer a year later in the 7th grade when he began writing his first story, and that book would be the beginning of the Ravin Saga Universe.

Roger's family moved back to South Dakota, where he finished high school and met his future wife Alysia. He enrolled at the University of South Dakota to study biology, chemistry, and creative writing. His plan was to go into veterinary medicine and be a small animal surgeon. However, it was in his creative writing classes that Roger realized his dreams. Finishing his first book in college, five more followed as he honed his storytelling skills.

Roger lives with his wife, son, two cats, two dogs, and a turtle he doesn't claim in small Gayville, SD. And yes, that really is the town's name, so get used to it. When not working at his day job, he spends every moment he can spare at writing his next novel.

More Information and Media Available at: **RavinSaga.com**

CPSIA information can be obtained
at www.ICGtesting.com
Printed in the USA
LVHW080858050723
751565LV00006B/44

9 780615 792255